Stadium Stories:
Georgia Tech Yellow Jackets

Stadium Stories™ Series

Stadium Stories:
Georgia Tech Yellow Jackets

Adam Van Brimmer

GUILFORD, CONNECTICUT
AN IMPRINT OF THE GLOBE PEQUOT PRESS

INSIDERS' GUIDE®

Text design: Casey Shain
All photos by Georgia Tech/Collegiate Images.
Cover photos: *front cover:* Daryl Smith; *back cover:* top, John Heisman; bottom, Tech defenders on Georgia ballcarrier

Library of Congress Cataloging-in-Publication Data
Van Brimmer, Adam.
    Stadium stories : Georgia Tech Yellow Jackets / Adam Van Brimmer.
    — 1st ed.
      p. cm. — (Stadium stories series)
    ISBN-13: 978-0-7627-4020-8
    ISBN-10: 0-7627-4020-5
      1. Georgia Institute of Technology—Football—History. 2. Georgia Tech Yellow Jackets (Football team)—History. I. Title. II. Series.
GV958.G43V35 2006
796.332'6309758231—dc22   2006041813

Manufactured in the United States of America
First Edition/First Printing

For Ann and Abigail, the lights of my world

Contents

Acknowledgments

I would like to thank Allison George and her staff in the Georgia Tech sports information department for their help and support. Without their cooperation and guidance, this project would have been nearly impossible. Allison opened her archives and put me in touch with all the right people. Even when she had no time, she made time.

I feel blessed to have met and talked with many former players and coaches for this book. Time cheated me out of seeing George Morris tackle, Pepper Rodgers kick, Eddie Lee Ivery run (and run and run and run) against Air Force, and Gary Lanier get sacked on his only pass attempt versus Notre Dame. Having listened to them describe those days and those games, though, I feel like I was there.

Jack Wilkinson encouraged me from the beginning. The author of several Georgia Tech books himself, he gave advice that helped carry me through what was a daunting task. His resources, particularly his insights and interviews with the late Bobby Dodd, were immensely helpful. He put me in touch with Richard Reynolds, who could teach a graduate course in Yellow Jacket history without looking at his notes.

Thanks again to my wife, Ann, my inspiration. She often calls me her "favorite writer." I hope I made her proud with this book. Mike Urban, my editor, showed patience throughout the project, something this first-timer couldn't appreciate more.

Introduction

Atlanta's best Saturday afternoons all start the same way: with a gold-and-white 1930 Ford Model A Cabriolet charging across the bright green grass of Georgia Tech's Grant Field.

The Ramblin' Wreck is the star of the preeminent pregame ritual in sports. It's better than any pyrotechnic or laser-light show. Even impartial observers and fans of other teams get goosebumps.

The Wreck symbolizes the spirit of Georgia Tech football. The car has character, just like the program and the men who have been a part of it.

Some men were blessed with talent and became legends, like coaches John Heisman and Bobby Dodd and players Joe Guyon and Eddie Lee Ivery.

Others came from humble backgrounds only to become heroes, from scrubs captain-turned-coach William Alexander to reserve halfback-turned-unlikely-playmaker Chappell Rhino.

Their deeds are celebrated on a handful of Saturdays every fall. The band plays a fight song so catchy that a leader of the Soviet Union once sang it, the Wreck motors out into the sunshine, and more than 50,000 fans stand, cheer, and remember.

They remember the Heisman shift and lopsided victories. They remember Coach Dodd dressed in his Sunday best, orchestrating the game plan from a folding chair. They remember stunning upsets over top teams, such as Joe Namath–led Alabama in 1962 and unbeatable Virginia in 1990.

They remember unbeaten streaks, national championships, and rival Georgia's "Drought" against their Yellow Jackets.

They remember, and they rejoice.

The Wizard of the Flats

John Heisman welcomed his Georgia Tech team to preseason practice with the same speech every year. "What is this?" began Heisman, referring to a football he held in his hands. "It is a prolate sphere, an elongated sphere in which the outer leather casing is drawn tightly over a somewhat smaller rubber tubing."

After a brief pause for effect he finished the thought: "Better to have died as a small boy than to fumble this football." The speech was overly dramatic, to be sure, expected from a man who moonlighted as an actor in summer stock theater companies. All the world—particularly football fields—was Heisman's stage during his thirty-six years of coaching, including sixteen at Georgia Tech.

His preseason speech was no act, however, as those who desecrated the football by fumbling it found out. Heisman sent them to the sidelines with orders to bounce a football off a fence bordering the practice field one hundred times, tucking it away snugly under their arm with each repetition.

This punishment, which he outlined in one of the earliest football manuals, his 1922 tome *Principles of Football*, worked best because he said it could "cure men of persistent faults much more quickly than any amount of scolding."

In many ways Heisman cured football of many of its early faults. The game didn't so much undergo an evolution during Heisman's days at Georgia Tech as it did a revolution—with Heisman leading the mob.

He was the catalyst behind the legalization of the forward pass; the innovator who introduced presnap offensive shifts, the power sweep, and the hidden-ball trick; and a proponent of skilled play by quick and athletic players, the kind who today win the award named in his honor, the Heisman Trophy.

And by sculpting the game in his image, he established one of college football's first powerhouses at Georgia Tech. Heisman posted a 102–29–7 record from 1904 to 1919 at Tech. He coached four undefeated teams, including the 1917 national

Loss of a Legend

John Heisman had few detractors among Georgia Tech followers during his sixteen-year tenure. One finicky fan eventually drove him off the Flats, though: his wife, Evelyn.

The Heismans split in 1919, and the coach announced his departure following a season-ending loss to Auburn. Heisman told reporters he and Evelyn were divorcing and that he had agreed to leave Atlanta. "Wherever Mrs. Heisman wishes to live, I will live in another place. This will prevent any social embarrassment." Evelyn stayed in Atlanta, and John returned to Philadelphia to coach at his alma mater, Penn.

William Alexander, a former player under Heisman and the legend's longtime assistant coach, took over the program. He carried on Heisman's success, posting a 23–4 record and winning league championships in his first three seasons. Alexander would coach twenty-five seasons and win a national championship.

Heisman's coaching career waned after he left Georgia Tech. His Penn teams went 16–10–2 in three seasons, and he posted a 7–2 mark in 1923 at Washington and Jefferson. He spent his final four years coaching at Rice. Those teams combined for a 14–18–3 record.

Heisman retired to New York City in 1928. He opened up a sporting goods store and founded the Downtown Athletic Club. The club awarded the first of what would become the Heisman Trophy in 1935 to University of Chicago star Jay Berwanger. Heisman died a year later, and the club named the trophy in his honor that year.

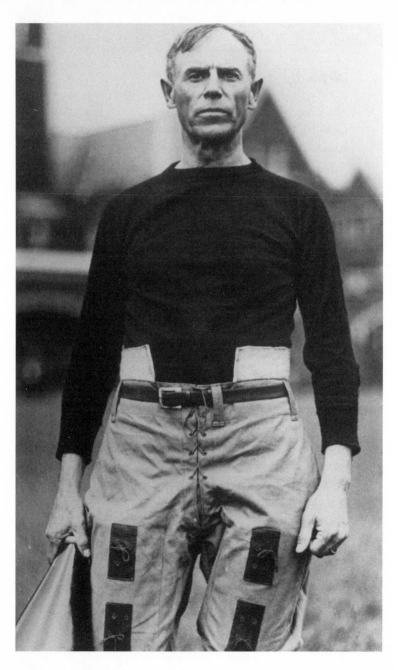

John Heisman, the wizard of the Flats.

championship team. He remains the winningest football coach in school history.

All by virtue of blind luck. Just months away from earning his law degree from the University of Pennsylvania, Heisman suffered eye trauma while playing a football game inside Madison Square Garden. The Garden featured galvanic lights, which could burn the eyes in much the same way as the sun.

Prolonged rest was the only treatment, and the team doctor recommended Heisman avoid straining his eyes for two years. The prescription made practicing law impractical—reading and writing were no-nos—so Heisman instead took a job coaching football following graduation.

He never did use his law degree. Heisman's coaching career began in 1892 at tiny Oberlin College in Ohio. He made stops at several other colleges over the next thirteen years, including the school now known as Auburn, as well as at Clemson University.

By the time he came to Georgia Tech, Heisman had already become one of the game's foremost innovators. He had invented the shotgun snap years earlier to make it easier on a particularly tall quarterback he coached at the school known today as Akron. Previously the center rolled or kicked the ball back to the quarterback rather than toss it back between his legs. At 6'4" his Akron quarterback struggled to bend over and pick the ball off the ground on every snap.

Heisman introduced the hidden-ball trick while at Auburn, using the play to score a touchdown against Vanderbilt. He also conceived the yardage marker and uniform numbers and was the first to instruct the scoreboard operator to post down and distance before each play.

But his real genius came out during his Georgia Tech tenure. First, he helped save the game. The cruel irony of Heisman's famous pregame speech is that men routinely died playing football—whether they fumbled or not—at the turn of the twentieth century. Protective equipment had yet to be introduced, and forward passing was illegal. Most offenses ran variations of two simple plays: the "buck," or run up the middle, and the "end run." Both produced brutal collisions.

During the 1905 season, Heisman's second on the Flats, eighteen players nationwide died from injuries sustained on football fields. The rash of deaths prompted President Theodore Roosevelt to threaten to outlaw the game. He told college administrators to make football safer, or else he'd pressure Congress to make playing the game a federal crime.

Coaches and administrators met in January 1906 in New York City. They proposed several new rules, all targeting the game's brutality. Shorten the game. Introduce the neutral zone at the line of scrimmage. Increase the distance needed to make a first down. Require six men on the line of scrimmage.

The most contentious of the proposed rules, however, was the legalization of the forward pass. Heisman pushed for it. He had long lobbied for its implementation, ever since witnessing a North Carolina fullback throw a desperation pass for a touchdown against Georgia in 1885—eight years before he would become a coach. And passing had always been a part of his offense in the form of laterals and backward passes.

One of his peers, Yale's Walter Camp, opposed passing. Camp is widely credited with molding football out of rugby in the late 1800s. Passing would change the integrity of the game,

Camp said. He suggested doubling the width of the field to open up the game.

Several schools, including Yale's rival, Harvard, had built stadiums by that time. Widening the field would be impractical. The coaches and administrators instead legalized the forward pass—albeit with several restrictions that would eventually be stripped away over the next ten years—and football's modern era began, thanks in large part to Georgia Tech's Heisman.

The forward pass succeeded in opening up the game, although Heisman didn't turn into an early-day Steve Spurrier upon its legalization. Quite the contrary, in fact, as he went on to revolutionize the running game with the "Heisman shift" and the pulling-guard play, the forerunner of the power sweep.

Heisman honed his strategy to the point that his teams became unstoppable in the late 1910s. During a three-season span between 1916 and 1918, Tech outscored the opposition 1,378–69. A powerhouse backfield led those teams. A handful of years before famed sportswriter Grantland Rice would immortalize Notre Dame's Four Horsemen backfield, Georgia Tech's quartet of Albert Hill, Joe Guyon, Everett Strupper, and Judy Harlan dominated the college game.

Guyon stood out from the others. An American Indian, he played at Carlisle Indian School with Jim Thorpe before coming to Georgia Tech. His talents prompted Heisman to get as creative with eligibility rules as the coach was with offensive strategy. Heisman wooed Guyon to Tech by setting him up with a job at the Ford plant near campus and hiring his brother Charlie as an assistant coach. Then Heisman convinced the NCAA to consider Carlisle a prep school, giving Guyon eligibility at Tech.

Guyon played for two years at Georgia Tech. The team won a national championship and went 15–1 during his playing career. He rushed for 344 yards on twelve carries in a win against Vanderbilt. Speed set him apart, and when asked about it years after his playing career ended, he gave away his secret. "When I was a kid, I heard a man say the only good Indian was a dead Indian, and from then on I was a pretty fast Indian."

John Heisman (holding megaphone) with his coaching staff.

Ralph McGill, a Pulitzer Prize–winning journalist and sportswriter at the *Atlanta Constitution*, would later write that "Joe Guyon is the greatest football player the South ever saw. He was almost a team by himself."

Tech's lone loss during Guyon's career marked one of the few times Heisman's creativity backfired. Coming off the 1917 national championship season, Heisman scheduled a game with another power team of the times, coach Pop Warner's Pittsburgh team. Heisman agreed to play at Pitt in 1918, 1919, and 1920.

Heisman's teams were hammered in the Steel City. Warner convinced the game officials that all of Heisman's presnap shifting was illegal. Too stubborn to adjust his strategy, Heisman kept shifting. The officials continued to call penalties. Pittsburgh won 32–0, ending Tech's thirty-three-game unbeaten streak. Pitt won the meetings the next two years as well.

The Pittsburgh games notwithstanding, Heisman had few lapses in wisdom during his heyday. And he lavished innovations on his players, particularly during his glory years at Georgia Tech. He came up with what he called basic "axioms of play"—175 of them. They included:

Don't try to play without your head.
Always win the game.
Never play less than your very hardest.
You can't win without knowing these principles.

He controlled every aspect of his team's training. He had twenty-one dietary rules, although not all of them made sense. He approved of all vegetables except cabbage—he gave no reason why—and demanded that all bread be stale or toasted. "No hot bread of any kind," he wrote in *Principles of Football*.

The Wisdom of John Heisman

Each newcomer to a Heisman-coached football team received a written list of principles from the coach. Heisman introduced them to the public in his 1922 book *Principles of Football*. They read:

ALWAYS
Always play with your head.
Always run your fastest.
Always tackle low.
Always be where the ball is.
Always win the game.

DON'T
Don't try to play without your head.
Don't see how light you can hit, but how hard.
Don't stop running because you are behind.
Don't "blow"; keep calm, cool, and determined—but FIGHT all the way.
Don't lose the game.

CAN'T
You can't make the team if you don't understand teamwork.
You can't do yourself justice without getting and staying in condition.
You can't afford to waste time talking.
You can't afford to loaf any during football season.
You can't win without knowing these principles.

NEVER
Never get excited.
Never give up.
Never play less than your very hardest.
Never come on the field without your brain.
Never forget a football player may be a gentleman.

Players were to limit their water intake during practice breaks to "half of a small dipperful at a time" because it is "impossible to do brilliant athletic work with a stomach full of water." And although players could drink as much water as they wanted after practice, they could take cold showers only—hot showers were reserved for game days.

He also dispensed medical advice, devoting a whole chapter of his book to the treatment of football injuries.

Heisman preached, "To break training without permission is an act of treason." Another form of discipline Heisman demanded from his teams was sportsmanship. He abhorred profanity almost as much as he did fumbling. And among his favorite axioms was "Never forget a football player may be a gentleman."

That axiom didn't always apply to the coach. Heisman didn't invent running up the score like he did the center snap and the power sweep, but he did refine the practice. His Georgia Tech teams scored more than 100 points against five opponents and broke the century mark three times in one season.

Heisman's 1916 Georgia Tech team scored the most lopsided victory in college football history. Tech beat Cumberland College 222–0 on October 7, 1916. The coach claimed he ran up the score to shame the pollsters, who awarded national championships at the time based largely on points scored without taking into account the strength of a team's opponents. But the press and fans knew that Heisman held a personal grudge against Cumberland.

Heisman's animosity against Cumberland dated to the previous spring, when the Tennessee college had defeated Heisman's Georgia Tech baseball team 22–0. Heisman later learned that the law student coaching the Cumberland team, George Allen, had recruited twenty-two professional players from Nashville. Allen needed a convincing win against Georgia Tech to persuade the school's new president to reconsider his decision to disband its athletic programs. Cumberland's once-proud teams were abysmal, and the new president stressed that the college should concentrate on its academic mission.

The resulting beatdown deeply bruised Heisman's pride, and he looked forward to a scheduled football game with Cumberland in 1916. The baseball rout failed to save Cumberland's athletic programs, though, and the president folded the football team. Cumberland sent Heisman a letter explaining the situation, but instead of scheduling another opponent, Heisman sent this reply: We'll pay your travel expenses and $500 to come and play, but if you don't show, I'll sue you for $3,000 for the lost gate receipts.

Heisman's letter eventually reached Allen, who had been the football team's student manager. Fearing the $3,000 demand would further turn the president against athletics—Allen continued to try to convince the school of athletics' merits even after the teams were disbanded—he decided to field a team and play the game. Allen promised a bunch of his law-school buddies a share of the $500 and a free train ride to Atlanta for the weekend if they played.

The takers found the deal to be a raw one. Georgia Tech scored 126 points in the first half, though that wasn't enough for Heisman. Never one for inspirational speeches—he loathed them, in fact—he gave one at halftime. "You're doing all right, but you just can't tell what those Cumberland players have up their sleeves," he told his players, reportedly with a straight face.

Cumberland did come out with a new game plan: Punt on every first down. Tech led 180–0 at the end of three quarters. Star halfback Everett Strupper, who would become the first national All-American from the Deep South a year later, scored six of Georgia Tech's thirty touchdowns in the game. *Atlanta Journal* reporter Morgan Blake summed up the game best in his written account of the game. "As a general rule, the only thing necessary for a touchdown was to give a Tech back the ball and holler, 'Here he goes' and 'There he goes.'"

Georgia Tech's offense totaled 978 yards, all on the ground. Tech did not attempt a pass. According to another published account, not all of Cumberland's players stayed for the onslaught. Two were discovered hiding under a blanket on the Tech bench, while a third jumped the fence and left the field during the game.

After the game mercifully ended, Heisman put his team through an additional thirty-minute scrimmage. Then he and the alumni bought all the players a steak dinner.

The Cumberland game was the second of the season for Heisman's team, which went on to finish with an 8–0–1 record. The next year Tech finished unbeaten for the third consecutive year and was awarded a share of the national title.

The Cumberland rout is just one example of the many contrasts in Heisman's coaching style. He was old-fashioned and conservative in many ways. "When in doubt, punt!" was a cornerstone of his coaching philosophy. Yet he remains among the most innovative coaches in history.

He made clear in his *Principles of Football* that the game's biggest contribution is the impact it has on young people. "Is it not of importance that a young man start out in life with an

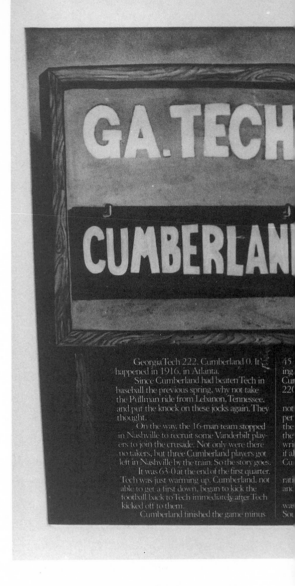

Georgia Tech defeated Cumberland 222–0 in 1916, which remains the most lopsided victory in college football history.

Georgia Tech 222. Cumberland 0. It happened in 1916, in Atlanta.

Since Cumberland had beaten Tech in baseball the previous spring, why not take the Pullman ride from Lebanon, Tennessee, and put the knock on these jocks again. They thought.

On the way, the 16-man team stopped in Nashville to recruit some Vanderbilt players to join the crusade. Not only were there no takers, but three Cumberland players got left in Nashville by the train. So the story goes.

It was 63–0 at the end of the first quarter. Tech was just warming up. Cumberland, not able to get a first down, began to kick the football back to Tech immediately after Tech kicked off to them.

Cumberland finished the game minus

ability to shut his jaws hard and say 'I will' or 'I will not' and mean it? Football is the game that will build up willpower in a boy's immature mind just about five times faster than anything else in this world."

ch had 528 yards rush-
koff returns and returned
zing punts for another
Tech did not throw a pass.
e South is about football.
v this game actually hap-
ohn Heisman (for whom
was named) allowed
merely to show sports-
un up muscular scores
were as easy as

riots that writers were
on their points scored.
r of their schedules.
1916, Georgia Tech
otball power in the

We remember. Because it reminds us
how hard we were working to make the
South a producer of steel. Just like it was
beginning to turn out strong football teams.
In 1916, U.S. Steel in the South was
known as the Tennessee Coal, Iron and Rail-
road Company. And while Tech was putting
it to Cumberland, 222-0, we were producing
steel ingots at one million tons a year—for
the first time. At our Fairfield Works in
Alabama.
And we had just authorized construc-
tion of a 45-inch blooming mill, and a combination bar and structural mill. At Fairfield!
Like John Heisman, the Pullman rail-
road car and the leather football helmet—
we go back a long way.
With the South.

Wrong-Way Run Right for Tech

The gold card denoted membership in the Georgia Tech Lettermen's Club. Roy Riegels studied it. For Riegels the card symbolized more than forty years of emotional memories. Nearly a half-century of pain and joy were written upon it as clearly as his name.

"Believe me," he told a room full of Tech alumni and boosters during a hall of fame induction ceremony on the afternoon of September 25, 1971, "I feel like I've earned this."

A man forever associated with a wrong was right. His ties to Tech did warrant a club membership, even though he never played football on the Flats.

Although the card bore only his proper name, "Roy Riegels," he's known by an unflattering nickname: "Wrong Way." He earned that moniker on New Year's Day, 1929, when, as a linebacker for the California Bears playing in the Rose Bowl, he scooped up a Georgia Tech fumble and returned it the wrong way.

Riegels was sport's original goat. Long before baseball player Bill Buckner let a ground ball roll between his legs in the World Series, basketball star Chris Webber called a time-out when his team didn't have one in the NCAA Tournament title game, or golfer Jean Van de Velde made a triple bogey when a double bogey would have won the British Open, Riegels recovered a fumble, lost his bearings, and dashed toward the wrong end zone.

That the gaffe happened in what was considered at the time the biggest football game of the year—college or pro—and led to a Georgia Tech victory and national championship only magnified its significance. The game was broadcast on radio nationally, and a sportswriter from nearly every major newspaper in the country witnessed it, along with the 70,000 fans on hand in Pasadena, California. Historians estimate newspapers devoted 450,000 column inches to the game and Riegels's blunder.

Most accounts portrayed Riegels as a buffoon, and his wrong-way run has become one of the most infamous plays ever in football. The January 2, 1929, issue of the *Chicago Daily Tribune* featured the headline BLUNDER DEFEATS CALIFORNIA: CAPTAIN

Cal's Roy Riegels returns a fumble the wrong way against Georgia Tech in the 1929 Rose Bowl. The play is among the most infamous in sports history.

ELECT RUNS 69 YARDS TO WRONG GOAL. Seventy-five years later, in 2004, a national magazine ranked the gaffe number six among the twenty biggest screw-ups in sports history—behind Buckner's error, Webber's mistake, and Van de Velde's choke. It has been parodied on television and movies and is referenced in religious devotions and on political bloggers' Web sites.

The story behind it, though, is both heartbreaking and uplifting. Riegels starred for Cal, one of college football's early powerhouses, in the late 1920s. A center and linebacker during an era of two-way players, Riegels earned All-American honors the year after his Rose Bowl miscue and went on to play professional football.

But in one excruciatingly long moment in the second quarter of the 1929 Rose Bowl, Riegels became "Wrong Way" Roy.

Georgia Tech had the ball on its own 23 yard line. Tech ran a misdirection play with halfback Stumpy Thomason, who made a long gain only to fumble the football at the end of the run. "I had gained up to our 35," Thomason said in published accounts. "Suddenly I was on the ground amid a great deal of commotion."

Trailing the play, Riegels picked the ball out of midair and turned to run. With players from both teams all around him, he turned toward the middle of the field. According to Bill Fincher, a Georgia Tech assistant coach, one of Riegels's teammates yelled at him, "Wrong way" to try to encourage him to keep going down the sideline. "In the confusion and with the open field in front of him, Riegels changed directions," Fincher said in *Ramblin' Wreck*, a history of Georgia Tech football.

Riegels refused to blame others for the gaffe. "I was running toward the sidelines when I picked up the ball," Riegels later told an Associated Press reporter. "I started to turn to my left toward Tech's goal. Somebody shoved me, and I bounded right off into a tackler. In pivoting to get away from him, I completely lost my bearings."

Cal's Benny Lom, a halfback, took off after Riegels and attempted to turn him around. But Riegels, thinking Lom wanted him to lateral the ball so a faster player could run with it, waved him off. "Get outta here, Benny. This is my ball!" Riegels afterward admitted he screamed at Lom. Lom finally grabbed Riegels by the hand and turned him around just short of the goal line, where several Georgia Tech players tackled him.

Each witness had a different take on the miscue. Broadcaster Graham McNamee, calling the game on the radio, asked a national audience, "What am I seeing? What's wrong with me? Am I crazy? Am I crazy? Am I crazy?" Tech coach William Alexander, meanwhile, uttered the antithesis of McNamee's frantic call. As Riegels took off the wrong way, Georgia Tech's reserves sprang off the bench and started cheering him on. The always low-key Alexander turned and ordered them to sit down. "He's just running the wrong way. Every step he takes is to our advantage," Alexander said. "Let's see how far he goes."

Riegels turned around inside the 5 yard line and was buried by Tech tacklers. The officials spotted the ball at the 1. California elected to punt rather than try to move the ball off the goal line—a common practice in those days—and Tech's Vance Maree blocked the kick. The ball hit a Cal player and rolled out of the end zone, giving Tech a safety and a 2–0 lead.

The turn of events left Riegels inconsolable at halftime. He initially refused to return to the field, telling coach Clarence Price through tears he'd ruined the game. "I couldn't face that crowd to save my life," Riegels reportedly told Price. The coach convinced Riegels otherwise, and "Wrong Way" made several tackles and blocked a kick in the second half.

Georgia Tech increased its lead to 8–0 early in the second half. Thomason scored on a run, but the Tech kicker missed the extra point. The missed PAT sealed Riegels's fate. Had the kick been good, the safety following Riegels's run would not have been the difference between winning and losing, as Cal scored a touchdown in the closing minutes. The final score: 8–7.

Riegels admirably dealt with reporters after the game,

Alexander the (Coaching) Great

Few coaches succeed in replacing a legend. The odds are even longer when the successor has no head coaching experience and is the polar opposite of his predecessor. William Alexander did more than just continue the legacy left by John Heisman at Georgia Tech, though.

He established his own tradition. Alexander's winning percentage of 58 percent fell well short of Heisman's. It also doesn't measure up to that of the man who succeeded Alexander on the Flats, Bobby Dodd. But for twenty-five years, Alexander maintained the program's national reputation, even as he coached players of inferior talent.

Notre Dame coach Knute Rockne, whose team faced Georgia Tech throughout the 1920s, summed up Alexander's coaching ability best by saying, "Bill Alexander gets more out of less than any coach in America."

Heisman coached Georgia Tech during football's infancy. Few college coaches nationwide, and even fewer in the South, could keep up with the game's evolution the way Heisman could. But by the mid-1920s the rest of the country had caught up. Rockne had the Four Horsemen at Notre Dame. Clarence Price coached a juggernaut at Berkeley. Wallace Wade was establishing a storied football tradition at Alabama.

Alexander coached two great teams in 1927 and 1928, winning conference titles both years and the national championship in 1928. But that season, capped by a victory over Cal in the Rose Bowl, would be Tech's last winning season until 1937. Dodd, who arrived at Tech as an assistant coach after a stellar playing career at Tennessee, once remarked that the Volunteers' third-stringers were more talented than Alexander's starters.

Yet Alexander survived the lean years by virtue of his classy approach and dedication to the school. By the time he retired following the 1944 season, he'd put the program on course to becoming a national power under Dodd's guidance. "No one else could have commanded the support of school, public, and players as did coach Aleck while losing so many games," Dodd said of his mentor.

Alexander spent forty-four years at Georgia Tech as a player, assistant coach, head coach, and athletic director. He was serving as athletic director when he died in his sleep on April 23, 1950.

Coach William Alexander, who went from scrubs team captain to national championship coach at Georgia Tech.

humbly telling his story. He quickly learned to live with it and over the years reached out to players who made similar mistakes.

A high school defensive lineman returned an interception the wrong way in 1957, resulting in a game-deciding safety. Riegels sent the player a letter, the contents of which were published by the Associated Press. The note closed with these words from Riegels: "For many years I've had to go along and laugh whenever my wrong-way run was brought up, even though I've grown tired listening and reading about it. But it certainly wasn't the most serious thing in the world. I regretted doing it, even as you do, but you'll get over it."

Riegels's laughter eventually became genuine. He, along with his teammate Lom, received an invitation to attend Georgia Tech's Hall of Fame luncheon in the fall of 1971. The Rose Bowl team was being inducted, Riegels was told, and because the team and Riegels were forever tied together, he should attend. He did, and after sitting through not one but two showings of his infamous run captured on grainy celluloid film, he came to the podium to receive his membership card.

"I was telling Stumpy [Thomason] I really was sore at him, because if he had never fumbled that ball it never would have happened," Riegels joked. Thomason replied by saying, "I feel like I made Roy Riegels famous."

Riegels failed to do the same for Thomason and Georgia Tech. His blunder overshadowed one of the great seasons in the early days of college football. As the female lead in the late 1990s movie *Tin Cup* told Roy McAvoy, a driving range pro–turned–U.S. Open contender, after McAvoy shot a thirteen on the final hole and lost the tournament to Peter Jacobsen, "Years from now, nobody will

Cast of Characters

College football fans will always remember the name of Roy Riegels for the Cal star's infamous wrong-way run in the 1929 Rose Bowl. Georgia Tech had its own cast of memorable characters who played in that game as well.

Fullback Roy "Father" Lumpkin arrived in Atlanta in 1927 straight from the Texas prairie and turned out to be an ornery cuss. He continually clashed with head coach William Alexander and turned pro following the national championship season. He joined a team in Portsmouth, Ohio, and became a fan favorite for his refusal to wear a helmet during games.

Lumpkin tried to convince one of his Tech backfield mates to come with him as well. Stumpy Thomason might have gone, if not for his relationship with Bruin, a young brown bear given to the team by an Atlanta businessman in honor of the team's victory over the Cal Bears. Thomason adopted the beast, taking Bruin for car rides around the city and supplying the bear with his two favorite dietary staples: beer and Coca-Cola.

According to the Tech dean of students at the time, George Griffin, Bruin was "at least as smart as most Tech students, with all of the vices of modern youth."

Bruin lived under the east stands of Grant Field. He often left his home to roam the campus and the nearby streets, and Atlanta police often received calls about the stray bear. The officers would pull up to Bruin, coax him into the back of their squad car, and return him to Tech.

remember who won the U.S. Open. But they'll always remember your thirteen."

Georgia Tech's 1928 season played out like a Hollywood script, going back to the final game of the 1927 season. Tech faced rival Georgia in the final. The Bulldogs were arguably the nation's best team in 1927, so good they had been dubbed the "Dream and Wonder" team by the media. Georgia had allowed just 27 points in its previous nine games combined and came to Atlanta the first Saturday in December undefeated and poised to accept a Rose Bowl berth.

Georgia Tech would turn the Bulldogs' season from dream to nightmare. Four weeks before the game Tech's Alexander split his team into two squads. One, made up mostly of reserves, would play the next three games. The other, comprised of the team's best players, would devote four weeks of practice to preparing for Georgia. "The Plan"—as Alexander referred to it—worked, as Tech beat Georgia 12–0 and denied the Dogs a Rose Bowl trip.

The next season Tech returned all but one of its key players, including Thomason and backfield mates Warner Mizell and Ronald Durant, as well as All-American linemen Peter Pund and Frank Speer. Alexander added three players off the freshman team in end Tom Jones, fullback Roy "Father" Lumpkin, and Maree, a tackle.

Pund remains among the most highly regarded linemen in Tech history. Said Notre Dame's Rockne of Pund following a 13–0 season-opening loss to Tech that season, "I counted twenty scoring plays that this man ruined. We were hopelessly beaten, but I had the thrill of my life to see great fighters go down in defeat before a greater fighter."

The Golden Tornado followed the Notre Dame wins with shutout victories the next two weeks. The team upped its record to 5–0 with wins against North Carolina and Oglethorpe.

The toughest two opponents on Georgia Tech's schedule vis-ited Atlanta the next two weeks. Vanderbilt was a power at the time, coached by the legendary Dan McGugin. One week after facing the Commodores, Tech would play host to Wallace Wade's Alabama team.

Tech beat Vandy 19–7, breaking the game open with a triple-reverse pass play Alexander had drawn up as a way to liven up practice sessions. Durant called the play, which culminated in a pass from Jones, the end, to Mizell, the quarterback, for a long touchdown.

"Funny thing, I had instructed Durant never to throw that play against a deep diamond defense," Alexander later told a biographer. "An interception and long runback were too likely. But the only time it ever worked was in that Vandy game, and Durant called it against a deep diamond defense with [a defensive back] in position to catch it and run 90 yards the other way. It goes to show how smart we coaches are."

Alexander confronted Durant afterward and was told, "Coach, I had tried everything else and nothing would go. There wasn't anything else to do."

Alexander's team members started to believe they were part of something special that day. So much so, in fact, that they appeared overconfident the next week against an inferior Alabama team. The Crimson Tide scored two touchdowns in the first half against a Tech defense that had allowed just three scores all season.

Tech's lax play prompted a rare locker room explosion from Alexander, a coach so reserved that intermission usually seemed more like naptime than halftime. His pregame speech before his head coaching debut in 1920 had contained just ten words: "It would be good to start off with a win."

Alexander was the original Tech man. He had left his home

in the Kentucky mountains to enroll in the school's civil engineering program in 1906. Without a proper high school education, he needed six years to graduate. He went on to become a math instructor at Tech and headed up the army's artillery training school during World War I.

Not blessed with size, speed, or talent, he became one of Heisman's "scrubs," known nowadays as the "scout team." By Alexander's third year, one of his teammates suggested to Heisman that the coach make Alexander the captain of the scrubs. "He's never absent, he's always trying, and he's always at the bottom of the pile," star player Chip Robert told Heisman.

In his role as captain of the scrubs, Alexander spent each Saturday scouting future opponents. Heisman so appreciated his efforts that the coach played Alexander in two games his senior year, enough for him to earn a letter. Alexander joined Heisman's coaching staff the next year and succeeded him in 1920. The contrast in the two coaches' personalities was palpable: Heisman the dictator handed off the Tech program to Alexander the diplomat.

Alexander morphed into Heisman at halftime of the Alabama game, though. He blistered his players, calling them "false alarms loafing in the limelight." Then he drew up a defensive scheme to stop Alabama's most effective play. Georgia Tech scored 20 unanswered points in the second half.

The Golden Tornado wrapped up its regular season by pasting Auburn in the traditional Thanksgiving Day game between the two schools and downing Georgia 20–6.

Tech's unbeaten, untied record earned the trip to Pasadena, although not without help. Two other southern teams were Rose Bowl contenders that season: Tennessee and Florida. The Volunteers knocked off Florida, led by quarterback Bobby Dodd—the same Bobby Dodd who would become a hall of fame coach with the Yellow Jackets.

Tennessee beat Florida but failed to defeat rival Kentucky. The Wildcats played the Volunteers to a scoreless tie. The Vols had a touchdown called back in the game, the officials ruling that the ball carrier stepped out of bounds.

The Rose Bowl bid went to Georgia Tech as a result. The Pasadena game was the only bowl in those days. The first incarnation of the Rose Bowl lasted just one year: 1902, with Michigan blowing out Stanford, 49–0. Football was a savage and brutal game at the turn of the century and fell out of favor with the public, so a polo match replaced football as the main attraction a year later. But when polo drew only 2,000 spectators, the Tournament of Roses committee turned to Roman chariot races.

Football returned permanently in 1916, and the Rose Bowl quickly became football's premier game. A crowd of 71,000 turned out for the 1929 game between Georgia Tech and Cal.

Tech came in as the favorite, even though Speer didn't play because of eligibility issues. Cal's record of 6–2–2 wouldn't stand up in today's Bowl Championship Series, but at that time the Bears were beyond question the best team on the West Coast. Many people, including the coach of a team Tech had beaten, thought them superior to Georgia Tech. "If Tech plays the way it did against us, it can win," Alabama's Wade said. "Otherwise California will be too much."

What Wade and everybody else failed to figure on was Riegels, whose wrong-way run turned out right for Georgia Tech.

In Dodd We Trust

Every head turned in unison, searching for the source of the shriek. "Is that the Big Whistle?" Don Ellis asked the player next to him on the Georgia Tech practice field. "Uh-oh." From the wooden observation tower high above the field, Bobby Dodd the delegator was about to become Bobby Dodd the educator.

"He was the Big Whistle," said Ellis, an end on the 1953 to 1955 teams. "That whistle didn't blow up there from the tower often. When it did, it always got our attention."

Dodd oversaw practice daily from his perch. He sat cross-legged in a folding chair, just watching. Often he'd entertain sportswriters up there. Seldom did he venture down to take an active role in practice. Dodd was one of the first head coaches to run his program like a chief executive officer does a corporation. He coached his coaches. They coached the players. The Big Whistle's whistle collected cobwebs from lack of use. When it sounded and its owner descended from the tower, something special often happened.

"It usually involved kicking," said Pepper Rodgers, a quarterback and placekicker in 1951, 1952, and 1953. "He could kick the quick kick with great accuracy, like he was throwing a pass." Dodd had been an adept punter—and quarterback—during his All-American playing career at Tennessee. As coach, he expected his kicker to be just as accurate. And when the kicker failed, the whistle blew, and down Dodd climbed. He'd set up a folding chair as a target and pepper it with kicks, amazing all witnesses.

"He was the kind of coach who you trusted whatever he told you," said George Morris, a College Football Hall of Fame linebacker who played for Dodd. "With him you knew he'd find a way to win." And win he did. Dodd won 71 percent of his games over a twenty-two-year head coaching career at Tech. He coached two unbeaten teams, including the 1952 national champions. Six others won nine or more games. Tech appeared in thirteen bowl games under Dodd and won nine, earning the coach the nickname "the Bowl Master."

Dodd made Georgia Tech into a national power in the 1950s, equal to the Nebraska teams of the 1990s, the Miami teams of the 1980s, and the Alabama teams of the 1960s. How did

The Bowl Masters

Bobby Dodd earned the moniker "the Bowl Master" by guiding Georgia Tech to eight straight bowl victories in his tenure and a 9–4 bowl record overall. Evidently he taught his assistants the keys to bowl success as well. Frank Broyles and Ray Graves, Dodd's offensive and defensive coordinators during the glory years of the early 1950s, coached teams to two bowl victories over Dodd's Yellow Jackets.

Broyles's Arkansas team ended Tech's run of eight straight wins in the 1960 Gator Bowl. Broyles was in his second season as coach of the Razorbacks and would go on to coach them to seven Southwest Conference titles and become the winningest coach in school history.

Graves's Florida team defeated Dodd in his final game, the 1967 Orange Bowl. Graves was the innovator of Tech's "monster defense," which featured a roving linebacker/safety. He spent ten years with the Gators, coaching Dodd's son, Bobby Jr., and Heisman Trophy winner Steve Spurrier during his tenure. Florida won 67 percent of its games under Graves.

he build a dynasty at an engineering school with a style of play foreign in the South? Short answer: He made football fun. Fun to watch. Fun to play. Fun to coach. He may have kept his distance from the daily workings at practice, but he remained close to his players. Whereas his peers' practice fields resembled a combat zone, Dodd's often resembled a summer camp. Dodd's Jackets rarely hit during the week. Practices were short and often included touch football games. Friday practices almost always featured a volleyball game.

Coach Bobby Dodd (far right) goes over plays with his team.

"The only thing he asked for was discipline," Ellis said.

Trust came naturally. The first people to profess it were Tennessee students. It was 1928, and Dodd had led the Volunteers to an upset victory at Alabama. The team traveled by rail, and as the train rolled into the station in Knoxville, Dodd's classmates unfurled a banner that read "In Dodd We Trust."

By 1956 the Tech faithful were ready to put the motto and Dodd's likeness on currency. He'd spent twelve seasons in Atlanta as the head coach and fourteen more as an assistant to William Alexander. Dodd had shattered the greatest myth of southern football: that a team must be big and strong to succeed. His teams featured small, quick players, and his offense was based around the "belly series," a forerunner of the triple-option offense. Georgia Tech won eight or more games every season between 1951 and 1956 and six bowls in those six years.

"He had talent, and he had some good coaches," said Rodgers, who would go on to a successful college and professional coaching career of his own. "I proved everything a man can prove in coaching: I proved I could win with good players and could lose with bad players. Coach Dodd didn't have many bad players."

Good players. Good coaches. And, many have said, good luck. Dodd's biography is entitled *Dodd's Luck*. His Tech teams were 45–33–8 in games decided by a touchdown or less, including a 16–6–3 mark during the six glory years from 1951 to 1957. Dodd always seemed to have the right answer, be it an impromptu play, a quick kick, or an intentional safety.

His success in the clutch had more to do with intelligence than luck, though. Dodd possessed a keen football mind, one noted all the way back to his high school days. He invented plays back then, something he continued to do during his career at Tennessee—much to the chagrin of his coach, Bob Neyland.

If a defense was keying on the run, Dodd would slip in the Kingsport play, a bootleg pass he'd drawn up as a high schooler in Kingsport, Tennessee. Another favorite against overly aggressive defenses was the running pass, in which the quarterback would toss the ball to a halfback on an apparent sweep. The halfback would throw it to an open receiver downfield.

Dodd would call for a quick kick on a muddy field or in third-down-and-long situations. His teams often pinned unsuspecting opponents in bad field position with the kicks. And if his team was stuck back on its goal line, he'd order his quarterback to take a safety. Better to give up 2 points and be allowed to kick off than surrender 6 or get caught in a field-position game.

"We beat SMU one year 6–4," said Rodgers, referring to a 1953 game. "We had the lead. He had me take intentional safeties. That's how smart he was."

The whole notion of "Dodd's luck" is exaggerated, said one of his biggest rivals and closest friends, Paul "Bear" Bryant. "Dodd's luck was really Dodd smart," Bryant said in his biography. Dodd's smarts didn't apply to books. He spent six years in high school, studying only athletics. He graduated, Dodd said in his biography, only after he struck a deal with the principal. The deal: Dodd had to buckle down the last half of his senior year and pass all his remaining courses. That would still leave Dodd two credits short, but the principal would give those to him so he could go to college.

"See, I'd planned to make high school football my career," Dodd said in his biography. "Well, I'd never had any idea of going to college." Fortunately for Dodd he had street smarts, knowledge gained in pool halls and sandlot playing fields almost from birth. He was born in 1909 in the Blue Ridge mountain town of Galax, Virginia. The youngest of four children—three of them boys—he was constantly trying to match his siblings in games and sports.

His competitive nature eventually led to gambling. The family had a pool table in its home, and Dodd developed an accurate cue stroke. The family moved to Kingsport, about 70 miles southwest of Galax, and left the pool table behind. Dodd resumed the hobby in Kingsport, though, hustling games at a young age. He would later gamble on golf, poker, and tennis, among other games. Anything he felt he had an edge in.

His calculating mind also paid off on the football field. "That was the thing people didn't understand about coach Dodd, that he played the percentages," Morris said. "He was lucky, no doubt about it. But he was calculating. He was always looking for an advantage."

Dodd also knew a sure thing when he saw it. And in 1931 he saw one in Atlanta. The previous fall Dodd had a serendipitous meeting with Georgia Tech assistant coach Mack Tharpe. Georgia Tech head coach William Alexander had charged Tharpe with scouting future opponents. Tech had a game with North Carolina that November, and Alexander dispatched Tharpe to Knoxville to scout the Tar Heels.

But the assistant's car broke down en route. By the time he reached the stadium, the game was over. Tennessee had won 9–7. Tharpe approached Coach Neyland with questions. Neyland pointed him in Dodd's direction. Dodd told Tharpe all about North Carolina's stunting defensive line.

Few college teams did that back then—stunting involves the ends and tackles crossing and looping around each other after the snap—and Dodd's insights helped Tech pull out a 6–6 tie with Carolina a week later.

Neyland would later rue putting Dodd and Tharpe together. Dodd wowed Tharpe, and his scouting report impressed Alexander. As soon as football season ended, rumors circulated about Dodd's future. Neyland wanted him for his coaching staff. So did Wallace Wade, who had just left Alabama for Duke.

Tech wanted Dodd too, and Chip Robert invited him to Atlanta for a meeting. Robert was a wealthy businessman and the most powerful member of Tech's athletic board. He'd played football for John Heisman and remained close to the program following graduation.

Dodd won over Robert during the meeting. He was offered $300 a month, a princely sum during the Great Depression. Dodd agreed, provided he could return to Tennessee and finish the basketball season. He would join the Tech staff the following March after the conference tournament, which was scheduled to be played in Atlanta.

Georgia Tech knocked Tennessee out of the tournament. Dodd intentionally missed the bus back to Knoxville and started work at Tech the next day. Dodd's decision to start his coaching career at Tech and not Tennessee was just another chapter in his contentious relationship with Neyland.

Dodd started it. He had snubbed Neyland's initial scholarship offer coming out of high school. He and Kingsport teammate Paul Hug, a wide receiver considered one of the best athletes in the South, decided to go to college together. Their two offers: Vanderbilt and Tennessee. They picked Vandy, which at the time boasted the better football program. Neyland had been at Tennessee just two years when Dodd and Hug graduated. Neyland was still laying the foundation of a program that would win 80 percent of its games and post nine undefeated regular seasons under the legendary coach.

Dodd and Hug went to play for the Commodores. They went through preseason practice. School hadn't started yet. Dodd admitted in his biography he was "having the time of my life." Just before classes started, though, the school checked all the freshman grades. Dodd's weren't good enough.

Dodd and Hug left Nashville. They hitchhiked to Atlanta to play for Georgia Tech. Again Dodd's grades disqualified him. So they went to Athens to inquire about playing for Georgia. The Bulldogs didn't have any scholarships available.

Dodd and Hug made plans to go to Macon and play for Mercer. John Dodd, Bobby's older brother, called Neyland in the meantime to see if he'd still take the two. Neyland agreed, provided Dodd and Hug were in Knoxville the next morning by 10 A.M. They made it, and an odd player-coach pairing began.

Neyland was a military man, a West Point graduate who served in World War I and later rose to the rank of brigadier general in World War II. His approach clashed with Dodd's free-wheeling style as a player. But Neyland's team won with Dodd. An injury opened up a starting spot on the 1928 team, and the Dodd era began. Tennessee went 27–1–2 over the next three years, with Dodd earning All-America honors during his senior season of 1930.

Bobby Dodd (in suit and hat, with hands on hips) always dressed dapperly on game days.

After the Volunteers' win against Vanderbilt in 1930, Edwin Camp of the *Atlanta Journal* called Dodd the greatest southern football player who ever lived. He put Dodd in the same class as Jim Thorpe, George Gipp, and Red Grange.

Dodd the coach took the same approach as Dodd the player when it came to Neyland, though. Given a choice, he wanted to

go elsewhere. But he subconsciously took many of Neyland's philosophies with him. Like Neyland, Dodd despised pregame speeches. He rarely gave them, and he discouraged players from getting too fired up before games. Morris recalls an instance when Dodd caught several Tech players jumping up and down during pregame in anticipation of the game ahead.

"That's not going to help you in the fourth quarter," Dodd told them. "Save your energy."

Neyland's disciplined approach rubbed off on Dodd as well. Both favored meticulous game preparation, with a plan for almost every situation. Dodd took Neyland's discipline to a new level on game day. He structured the way the players stood on the sideline. He sat at a folding table on the 50 yard line, with his offensive players lined up shoulder-to-shoulder on one side and defenders on the other.

One of the Neyland game principles Dodd agreed with was "Conservative in the main, gamble when necessary." Dodd subscribed to that, particularly in bad weather or with his team in poor field position. Dodd didn't bring Neyland's smash-mouth football with him to Georgia Tech, though. Quite the opposite, in fact. Tech's teams were dismal during Dodd's first few years, depleted by financial constraints. By the late 1930s, however, Tech was recruiting athletes again, many of them basketball players. Dodd convinced Alexander to throw the ball more, and the open offense revived the program.

The Yellow Jackets went 6–3–1 in 1937, their first winning season since the 1928 national championship season. They went 8–2 in 1939, and Camp wrote in his biography of Alexander, titled *Alexander of Georgia Tech*, "If ever there was a coaching masterpiece, it was the Old Man's leadership and planning with a squad that offered only speed, intelligence, and determination as substitutes for power and individual prowess." Three years later, with Clint Castleberry in the backfield, Tech started 9–0 and finished 9–2.

Alexander's health began to fail in 1942, and Dodd assumed

a more active role. He worked as interim coach for two games that season and established himself as Alexander's eventual successor. And in 1945 he became Tech's coach. The football program and college football in general would soon change forever.

Dodd retired from coaching in 1966. Tech started that season 9–0 behind quarterback Kim King, "the Young Left-Hander." The Jackets lost the last two games of that season, though, falling to rival Georgia and third-year coach Vince Dooley in the regular-season finale and to Florida in the Orange Bowl.

Dodd submitted his resignation a month later, frustrated by the recruiting difficulties Tech faced because of its academic standards and pained by a chronic prostate-kidney condition.

It took Georgia Tech more than two decades to fill the coaching void left by Dodd. Four coaches followed him over the next twenty years, the best season a 9–2–1 finish in 1985.

Bobby Ross took over in 1987 and reestablished Tech's football reputation. His 1990 team won the school's fourth national title.

Dodd's retirement resonated elsewhere as well. Alabama's Bryant called Dodd the best game coach he'd ever known. King, the quarterback on Dodd's final team and a color analyst on Tech radio broadcasts for more than thirty years, said Dodd was the smartest man he'd ever known in the coaching profession.

Even coach Wally Butts, Dodd's nemesis at Georgia for most of his career, acknowledged Dodd's genius. "If Bobby Dodd were trapped at the center of an H-bomb explosion, he'd walk away with his pockets full of marketable uranium."

The Big Whistle indeed.

Winning Is Contagious

The greatest sign of desperation is to embrace that which we despise. Out of options, having exhausted every favored tactic, we turn elsewhere for help. Be it tough love with a child, a support group or a rehab center for an addict, or an experimental treatment by a doctor, what was once considered a final resort becomes a viable approach.

Bobby Dodd's spring of desperation came in 1951. Six seasons into what would become one of the greatest head coaching careers in college football history, Dodd's frustration with the talent level and inconsistent play of his Georgia Tech football team peaked. Years later he would tell his biographer, Jack Wilkinson, he considered leaving Tech following a 5–6 season in 1950. The coach recounted a telephone conversation he had with his brother, John, shortly after that season. "I told John I was either going to have to quit or go to another school," Dodd said in his biography, *Dodd's Luck*.

Instead he tried something even more desperate in his eyes: extending spring practice to six weeks. Dodd abhorred football's annual rite of spring. He disliked practice in general. He included volleyball games and touch football scrimmages in his practice plans during the regular season. He once told one of his former players, George Morris, that if he could turn his team over to Bear Bryant at Kentucky or Johnny Vaught at Mississippi during the week and he could coach the team on Saturday, the Yellow Jackets would never lose. "Those guys can prepare teams better than anybody, and I can figure out the guys on the other sideline," Dodd told Morris.

Coaching spring drills was the worst form of torture for Dodd. He often let his veteran players out of practice, telling them, "How much can we improve you? Two percent? And risk injury? No. Stay in shape and take practice off." Nobody heard that speech in the spring of 1951, though. The 1950 season was one of only two losing campaigns in Dodd's twenty-two years on the Flats. Injuries sidelined four starters midway through that season, a devastating blow in an era when team members played both offense and defense. Their absence contributed to a four-game losing streak, the longest in Dodd's tenure. A humiliating 54–19 home loss to rival Alabama capped that stretch.

Dodd despised losing even more than he despised practice. So following the 1950 debacle, he dismissed his two top assistants and close friends, Ray Ellis and Dwight Keith. He called the firings "the most depressing thing I ever had to do" in his biography. He wanted a younger coaching staff, though, to implement drastic changes in the spring.

He promoted line coach Ray Graves to the position now known as defensive coordinator and hired former Tech star Frank Broyles to oversee the offense. Graves's first suggestion was to install the "monster defense," which employed a rover in the defensive backfield.

Dodd charged Broyles, meanwhile, with devising an offense revolving around the "belly series," a forerunner of the triple-option play Dodd picked up on while serving as an assistant coach at a college all-star game. One of Dodd's quarterbacks in the game, Pacific's Eddie LeBaron, showed the coach the play.

With new schemes to implement, Graves and Broyles lobbied Dodd to adopt the two-platoon system. The idea of specialization was in its infancy in those days, with most teams still playing "Iron Man" football. Dodd agreed to slowly phase out two-way players.

The coaches were ready for spring practice. The players weren't. Dodd shocked his team on the first day of practice when he told team members they were to report to Rose Bowl Field every afternoon for the next six weeks. More surprises—the new schemes, two-platoon football—were still to come.

Bobby Dodd (center) talks with the staff of his 1952 national championship team.

Morris compares that spring to Bear Bryant's first camp at Texas A&M, immortalized in the book *The Junction Boys*, and to Arizona State coach Frank Kush's three-a-day workouts at Camp Tontozona. "Bear Bryant took his team to the desert, and Frank Kush took his to the mountains," Morris said. "We went to Rose Bowl Field."

The practices were short—ninety minutes to two hours—but hard. Full-contact scrimmages, another Dodd no-no, replaced the volleyball and touch football games. "By the end we knew who looked good in a uniform but couldn't play," Morris said. "That spring weeded out a lot of those guys."

That spring also launched one of the great runs in Georgia Tech history. Every act of desperation performed by Dodd—the coaching changes, the new schemes, the two-platoon system, even the extended weeks of practice—combined to create a wonder drug that cured the ills of 1950, a trying season that quickly proved beneficial. The injuries suffered midway through the 1950 season allowed several underclassmen to gain experience.

Scarred by all the losses in their debut season, Morris, Ray Beck, Hal Miller, and others were hungry for success when they reported for spring practice in 1951. With veteran tackle Lamar Wheat providing leadership, 1951 would dawn what is known as "the Golden Era" of Georgia Tech football.

Or, as Dodd put it in his biography: "I could finally see some daylight after the gloom of the previous year. . . . The sun came out. Boy, it came out from behind a dark cloud."

The dark cloud stayed away for more than two seasons. The Yellow Jackets didn't lose a game until the sixth week of the 1953 season. The thirty-one-game unbeaten streak, which began with wins in the final two games of 1950, is the second-longest in Tech history and established Dodd and the Georgia Tech program as one of the nation's best in the post–World War II era.

Here is a game-by-game look at that streak.

1950 Season

Georgia Tech 46, Davidson 14 (November 25). A Tech team bitter from the 54–19 loss to Alabama the previous week and the seven-degree temperature at Grant Field routed Davidson. The streak had begun.

Georgia Tech 7, Georgia 0 (December 2). An accurate scouting report helped Tech beat Georgia in Athens for the first time since 1916. The Yellow Jacket defense knew the Bulldogs' play before the snap based on the hand position of the right tackle and where the halfback lined up. The game likely would have ended in a tie had not Georgia's Lukie Brunson fumbled on his own 3 yard line. Tech recovered, and rookie quarterback Darrell Crawford scored on a quarterback sneak.

1951 Season

Georgia Tech 21, Southern Methodist 7 (September 22). Each member of Tech's trio of sophomore backs, Glenn Turner, John Hicks, and Leon Hardeman, scored a touchdown as the Yellow Jackets upset SMU. The Mustangs gave Tech early momentum, botching a punt snap inside their own 10 yard line midway through the first quarter to set up Tech's first score. The early lead bolstered the Jacket defense, which shut down SMU's star quarterback Fred Benners. "Their pass defense was good, and since that was the strong point of our offense, we had trouble getting going," SMU coach Rusty Russell said.

Georgia Tech 27, Florida 0 (September 29). Tech beat Florida for the fourth straight year since the two rivals resumed their series in 1948. Following the game Dodd paid his team what for him was a big compliment. "We might have a better football team than I thought we had," he said.

Georgia Tech 13, Kentucky 7 (October 6). Dodd was never one to bend an official's ear during a football game. He made an exception this day, however, remaining on the field at halftime to talk to the men in stripes about the rough play in the first half. Dodd later relayed the conversation to his players. "If you don't get this game under control, I'm going to turn my boys loose," Dodd told the officials. Tech halfback Johnny Hicks broke loose early in the second half, scoring on a 69-yard run. The Jackets failed on the conversion, however, and trailed 7–6. Kentucky coach Bear Bryant gave Georgia Tech a chance to win late in the game. Facing fourth-down-and-1 with the ball deep in Kentucky territory, Bryant sent his punt team onto the field. He changed his mind before the play, though, and put his offense back out there. Moments later the Wildcat running back slipped and fell in the backfield, and Georgia Tech took over on downs. Tech's Crawford threw a touchdown pass on the next play as Tech won 13–7.

Georgia Tech 25, Louisiana State 7 (October 13). The Yellow Jackets posted an easy victory, but the game is well remembered by players because it was played with a rubber football. Dodd moonlighted as a product representative for Voit, and the company asked him to use one of its new rubber footballs in a game. The ball proved slippery and hard to handle — except for linebacker George Morris. He intercepted two passes in the game.

Georgia Tech 27, Auburn 7 (October 20). The Yellow Jackets stretched an unbeaten streak against Auburn to eleven years thanks to Buck Martin's four touchdown catches on the Kingsport play. Dodd attended high school in Kingsport, Tennessee, and one of his favorite plays was a play-action bootleg pass to his best friend, Paul Hug. The play called for the quarterback to fake a toss sweep to the halfback and spin out to his right. The receiver, meanwhile, was to fall to his hands and knees on the snap as if to block, get up, and sprint toward the corner of the end zone. Provided the defense bought the fake to the left and over-pursued the run, the receiver should be wide open. Dodd installed the play the week before the game, recounting in his biography how Auburn's aggressive defense was geared to stop all of Tech's regular plays. Crawford, the Yellow Jacket quarterback, repeatedly set up the Kingsport play with off-tackle runs against Auburn. Martin scored on catches of 14, 13, 73, and 31 yards, burning an Auburn safety who would go on to become one of the biggest foils in Tech football history: Vince Dooley. Martin's four touchdowns tied a school record that stood for another twenty-one years.

Georgia Tech 8, Vanderbilt 7 (October 31). The Nashville mud proved the toughest opponent for both teams. The field was such a quagmire that the only way to tell Tech players from Vandy players was by the black strip on the crown of the Vandy helmets. Fullback Glenn Turner scored the Yellow Jackets' lone touchdown early in the game, but the mud led to a missed extra point. Vanderbilt had a 7–6 lead in the fourth quarter when Tech's Ray Beck tackled the punter in the end zone for the deciding safety.

Georgia Tech 14, Duke 14 (November 3). This game disproved the theory that a tie is as good as a loss. The Yellow Jacket players describe it as a "fortunate" tie against a good Duke team led by Worth "A Million" Lutz. Crawford scored Tech's only offensive touchdown on a quarterback sneak. The Jackets' other score came on a blocked punt return. Wheat blocked it into the arms of Beck, who ran 60 yards for a touchdown and a 14–7 lead. Lutz tied the game late, though, with his second scoring run of the game. "They controlled the ball, and if you can't have the ball you can't score," Dodd told reporters afterward. "That was the story of the game to me."

Georgia Tech 34, Virginia Military 7 (November 10). Losing to VMI in 1950 was almost as humiliating to Dodd as suffering the blowout loss to Alabama. But it also kept the Jackets from looking past Virginia Military to the rematch with the Crimson Tide the next week. Tech built a big early lead, allowing Dodd to rest his stars for the following week's game.

Georgia Tech 27, Alabama 7 (November 17). In the ultimate revenge game Dodd showed mercy. Alabama had humiliated Georgia Tech 54–19 at Grant Field the year before, and the Jacket players wanted vengeance before a partisan Alabama crowd in Birmingham. "They'd torn us apart," Morris said. "We asked coach Dodd to let us go because they'd beaten us so badly. But he said, 'No, we still have to play the University of Georgia.'" The Jackets won 27–7 behind Crawford, who threw for two touchdowns and ran for another. Dodd admitted in his biography he "called 'em off" that day, no doubt causing former Tech coach John Heisman, who had avenged a baseball loss to Cumberland

College with a 222–0 pummeling on the football field in 1916, to do a few barrel rolls in his grave.

Georgia Tech 48, Georgia 6 (December 1). The Yellow Jackets achieved what players still call the best first half of football ever played by a Tech team. They led 34–0 at the break, at the time the largest halftime margin in the history of the series. Tech's coaches had scouted the Bulldogs perfectly, just as they had the year before. Tech intercepted Georgia quarterback Zeke Bratkowksi eight times, a Southeastern Conference record at the time. Defensive back Larry Morris picked off one of those passes and returned it for a touchdown. The victory earned Georgia Tech a share of the SEC title with Tennessee and an Orange Bowl bid.

Georgia Tech 17, Baylor 14 (January 1, Orange Bowl). Long before the Orange Bowl stadium in Miami became known for the "wide right" and "wide left" field goal misses by Florida State kickers, the venue made a legend of Georgia Tech kicker Pepper Rodgers. The rookie kicker's 6-yard game-winner was the first field goal ever to decide an Orange Bowl and capped a second-half surge by the Yellow Jackets. "Boy, I sure would hate to go through that again," guard Ray Beck told reporters afterward. Tech rallied from behind twice in the game, first early on and then in the fourth quarter. Crawford hit Martin on the same play that had beaten Kentucky earlier in the season to tie the game with six minutes to go. Dodd elected to kick the extra point and tie the game rather than go for two and the win. Defensive end Pete Ferris gave Tech another chance later, though, intercepting a pass from Baylor's All-America quarterback Larry Isbell and returning it to the 9 yard line to set up Rodgers's kick. Tech triumphed despite being out-gained by over 100 yards. The win marked Dodd's second over a George Sauer–coached team in the Orange Bowl. Dodd's Jackets had defeated Sauer's Kansas Jayhawks in the 1948 game.

1952 Season

Georgia Tech 54, the Citadel 6 (September 20). Dodd had a way of making routs memorable. But this time rubber balls and multiple interceptions weren't necessary. The coach had the public-address announcer call Cecil Davis, a freshman defensive back who didn't dress for the game, out of the stands to play in the second quarter. Davis intercepted a pass in the second half as Tech opened its national championship season with a victory.

These six members of the 1952 national championship team made first-team All-America.

Georgia Tech 17, Florida 14 (September 27). Rodgers kicked his second-most-famous field goal as Tech rallied for victory in the fourth quarter. Bill Brigman, who succeeded Crawford at quarterback, set up Rodgers's heroics with a touchdown pass to Jeff Knox. Dodd later admitted that he predicted Rodgers would kick the game-winner, just as Rodgers had in the Orange Bowl the previous season.

Georgia Tech 20, Southern Methodist 7 (October 4). Rookie half-back Bill Teas's breakout game came in Dallas. Teas and Leon Hardeman, who played in the same backfield at Chattanooga's Baylor High School before arriving in Atlanta, combined to rush for 246 yards in the victory. Teas had almost 200 of those as well as three touchdowns. Two years later Teas would be within a yard of breaking the school's career rushing record when he missed curfew and was suspended from the team by Dodd.

Georgia Tech 14, Tulane 0 (October 11). Teas, Hardeman, and three others combined to run for over 400 yards against Tulane. The quintet of underclassmen became known as the "Rambling Rookies." Meanwhile, Tech's defense began a string of three consecutive shutouts.

Georgia Tech 33, Auburn 0 (October 18). Tech's defense proved a good offense against the rival Tigers. Defensive back Bobby Moorhead intercepted two passes and returned them both for long touchdowns. Moorhead went on to earn All-America honors that season. The shutout boosted Tech's standing in NCAA statistics. The Jackets were second in the nation in points allowed, allowing 27 combined in their first five games.

Georgia Tech 30, Vanderbilt 0 (October 25). Hardeman ran for over 100 yards, and Tech's defense posted a third straight shutout, something the Jackets have done only one time since—during the 1956 season.

Georgia Tech 28, Duke 7 (November 1). The game featured two unbeaten teams both ranked in the top ten. It failed to live up to that billing, though, as Tech jumped out to a 21–0 halftime lead. Duke ended Tech's shutout streak with a second-half touchdown, but the game still catapulted the Yellow Jackets onto the national stage. The victory earned a write-up in a national magazine, with Duke head coach Bill Murray calling the Jackets "the greatest team in the country." Several bowl scouts attended the game in Durham, North Carolina.

Georgia Tech 45, Army 6 (November 8). Dodd announced that his team had been offered a Sugar Bowl bid after this victory, which players say was much more lopsided than the score indicates. "It could have been 100–0," Morris said. Dave Davis's 80-yard punt return for a touchdown highlighted the game. Army coach Earl Blaik, whose Cadets dominated in the 1940s behind the backfield of Glenn Davis and Doc Blanchard, said of Tech: "I never compare teams, but this team could play in any league."

Georgia Tech 7, Alabama 3 (November 15). Alabama had everything: Wallace Wade coaching on the sideline, the great Bobby Marlow in the backfield, and legendary broadcaster and Tide alum Mel Allen in the broadcast booth. Little Jakie Rudolph broke all their hearts in the fourth quarter when he stopped Marlow—an orphan from Troy, Alabama, whom many consider

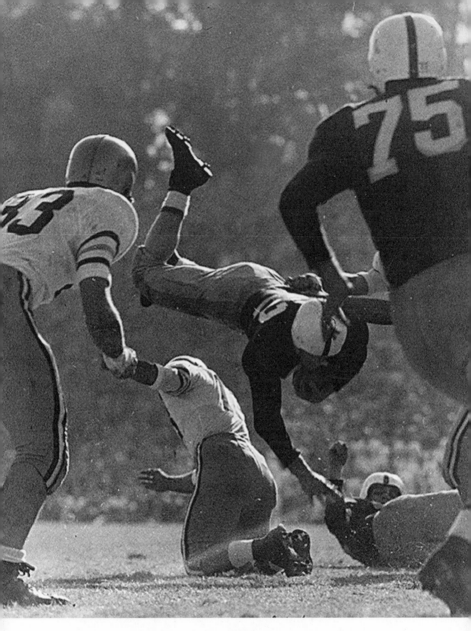

Georgia Tech's Jakie Rudolph (in white jersey, on knees) trips up Alabama's Bobby Marlow in what is known as the "$125,000 tackle."

one of the greatest runners in the history of the South—short on fourth down near the goal line. Rudolph, a 155-pounder, came up from his safety position to fill a hole at the line of scrimmage and flip Marlow. The infamous stop became known as the "$125,000 tackle" because it secured Tech's spot in the Sugar Bowl, which paid each of its participants $125,000.

Georgia Tech 30, Florida State 0 (November 22). The score might not reflect it, but the Yellow Jackets had a letdown in the game sandwiched between the rematch with Alabama and the rivalry game with Georgia. Dodd assessed his team's play in the shutout of the Seminoles as "just fair."

Georgia Tech 23, Georgia 9 (November 29). Tech traveled to Athens without Teas and Hardeman, who were out with injuries, and appeared ripe for an upset. The Jackets' Chappell Rhino earned the nickname "One-Play Rhino" instead. Rhino, a senior safety, threw an improvised touchdown pass on fourth down in the third quarter. Tech trailed 7–3 at the time, and Rhino, who hadn't even worked on the play in practice before, lined up at halfback, took a pitch from Rodgers, and lobbed a 10-yard strike to Martin. Dodd related his conversation with Rhino in his biography. "I took Chappell Rhino and asked him, 'Now, Chappell, you can throw the running pass, can't you?' He said, 'Oh yeah, coach.' I don't think he'd ever thrown one in a game. . . . But I thought Chappell was enough of an athlete where he could do it for me." The Bulldogs pulled to within a point later in the quarter when Rodgers intentionally took a knee in the end zone for a safety. But Moorhead gave Tech a more decisive lead when he picked off a pass from Bratkowski—the same Georgia passer who had thrown eight interceptions the year before—and returned it to the 1 yard line to set up a score.

Georgia Tech 24, Mississippi 7 (January 1, Sugar Bowl). The Yellow Jackets couldn't believe what they saw in the locker room at halftime of the Sugar Bowl. Perched on the training table, with

Leon Hardeman (11) fights to the end zone in Georgia Tech's 1953 Sugar Bowl win over Mississippi.

his legs swinging back and forth and his hands wrapped around a bottle of Coca-Cola, was Bobby Dodd. "Looks like we have them on the run," Dodd told his team. The score: 10–7. Ole Miss had opened the game by driving for a touchdown on its first possession, no doubt fired up by comments made by Dodd in the leadup to the game. Dodd wanted to play Syracuse or at least a

national opponent such as Texas, rather than an SEC foe, in the Orange Bowl that season, and he didn't hide it. Tech started sluggishly anyway after rain forced the Jackets to practice all week in an indoor facility with ceilings so low they couldn't throw a pass. Mississippi drove down inside the Tech 10 yard line on its second and third possessions as well, but the defense held both times. Morris made a tackle on fourth down at the 1 yard line on one of those possessions, and Tech rallied to take a 10–7 lead by halftime. Mississippi's coach, John Vaught, started his second team in the second half, and true to Dodd's word, Tech had the Rebels on the run. With the victory the Jackets completed a 12–0 season. The victories came by a combined score of 325–59.

End of the Streak

The record books state that Notre Dame snapped Georgia Tech's thirty-one-game unbeaten streak, the top-rated Irish defeating the number four Yellow Jackets 27–14 on October 24, 1953. But southern racism contributed as well.

Tech coach Bobby Dodd and Notre Dame's Frank Leahy originally had agreed to play the game in Atlanta. The game site changed, though, after Dodd learned that Leahy's team featured two black players. Desegregation was still years away, and whites didn't play against African Americans in the South. Fearing for his team's safety in a game played at Grant Field, Leahy telephoned Dodd and explained the problem. "See you in South Bend," Dodd told Leahy.

The Notre Dame matchup wasn't the first Yellow Jacket game impacted by southern prejudice. Nineteen years earlier Georgia Tech had gone to Ann Arbor, Michigan, to play the Wolverines. Tech nearly returned to Atlanta without playing the game. Michigan had a black player, Willis Ward, and Jacket coach Bill Alexander told Wolverine coach Fielding Yost his team couldn't play against Ward.

The two argued and debated the issue for hours before finally reaching a settlement the night before the game. If Yost held Ward out of the game, Alexander would bench his best player, end Hoot Gibson. Michigan went on to win 9–2 in a game Alexander described as "probably as poorly played a game between two major college teams as I've ever seen." Tech and Michigan haven't played each other since.

The color barrier finally fell as it pertained to the Yellow Jackets in the 1956 Sugar Bowl. Georgia Tech faced Pittsburgh, who had a black player, Bob Grier. Georgia's governor, Marvin Griffin, opposed Tech playing the Panthers the week before the game. The chairman of the board of regents eventually stepped in and told Georgia Tech it could play.

Grier ended up as the game's goat, committing an interference penalty near the goal line. That penalty allowed Tech to score the only touchdown in the 7–0 victory.

The loss of home-field advantage wasn't the only factor in Georgia Tech's streak-ending loss to Notre Dame in 1953. Quarterback Pepper Rodgers got hurt on the opening kickoff, forcing freshman Wade Mitchell into the starting role. Then Notre Dame's Leahy suffered a heart attack at halftime and was rushed to the hospital. Tech players remember well the scene outside the locker rooms before coming out for the start of the second half.

"Both teams used the same tunnel, and we came out of the locker room first and were standing in the tunnel when Notre Dame's players walked up behind us," linebacker George Morris said. "We heard them sniffling, and I turned around and looked: They were bawling. I knew we were in for a tough second half."

Tech scored first, tying the game at 7–7. Notre Dame retook the lead 14–7 later in the quarter and sealed the victory by recovering an errant snap in the end zone.

1953 Season

Georgia Tech 53, Davidson 0 (September 19). The football coaches association rules committee changed the substitution rules prior to the 1953 season, essentially outlawing two-platoon football. That change didn't matter in the opener, though, as Tech beat Davidson for the twelfth straight and final time.

Georgia Tech 0, Florida 0 (September 26). A hurricane in the Gulf of Mexico dumped driving rain in Gainesville throughout the game, making for a slippery ball. Hardeman fumbled twice inside the Florida 10 yard line as a result, and Tech was shut out for the first time since the 1949 season. Gator quarterback Doug Dickey had similar troubles holding onto the ball, giving away his team's best scoring opportunity with a fumble at Tech's 28 yard line.

Georgia Tech 6, Southern Methodist 4 (October 3). Dodd spoiled SMU's upset bid with some clever strategizing late in the game. SMU trailed 6–0 but continually pinned Georgia Tech deep in its territory. Dodd elected to yield safeties rather than field position, twice ordering his quarterback to take a knee in the end zone. The safeties gave Tech free kicks from its 20 rather than punts out of its end zone.

Georgia Tech 27, Tulane 13 (October 10). The unbeaten streak reached thirty games as Tech returned to New Orleans and the scene of its Sugar Bowl triumph the year before. Tulane would go on to finish last in the Southeastern Conference with a 1–8–1 overall record.

Georgia Tech 36, Auburn 6 (October 17). Auburn lost to Georgia Tech for the twelfth consecutive year in Atlanta. "It looked like we had a good day against Auburn all the time," Dodd said in his biography. "Didn't seem to matter how good they were." The Yellow Jackets would beat Auburn again the next season, but the 1953 victory over the Tigers would be the last in Tech's unbeaten streak. The Jackets lost 27–14 to Notre Dame the next week in South Bend.

The Drought Makers

You can rave about your Sinkwich
And Trippi's praises sing,
While talk about the "Bowl Days"
Still makes the welkin ring.

But to all Bulldog supporters
In every precinct in the South,
I propose a hearty toast
To the man who broke the drouth!

Rise up you loyal Georgians
From Tybee Light to Rabun Gap,
Here's to the Macon Mauler,
The mighty Theron Sapp.

I have seen some lovely paintings
In galleries of art,
Gorgeous sunsets on the water
Which stirred the inner heart.

But of all the wondrous visions
Ever seen by eyes of mine,
I'll take old number forty
Crashing through that Jacket line.

And so down through the ages
Whenever Bulldogs meet,
Whether in the peaceful countryside
Or on a crowded street,

The word will still be carried
By every loyal mouth —
Let's stand and drink another toast
To the man who broke the drouth!

— "The Man Who Broke the Drought" by Harold M. Walker

Theron Sapp is among the most celebrated Georgia Bulldogs of all time. His jersey number — 40 — is one of four retired by the school, along with Frank Sinkwich's number 21, Charley Trippi's number 62, and Herschel Walker's number 34. Unlike the other three, though, Sapp wasn't an All-American or a Heisman Trophy winner or finalist.

Sapp broke "the Drought," an eight-year losing streak to rival Georgia Tech, and that qualified him for legend status. Harold M. Walker penned "The Man Who Broke the Drought" the day after Sapp recovered a fumble and scored a touchdown in Georgia's 7–0 victory over the Yellow Jackets at Atlanta's Grant Field. Georgia retired his jersey two years later.

"The Drought" made legends at Tech as well. If Sapp is the "Drought Breaker," they are the "Drought Makers." They played during what is called "the Golden Era" of Georgia Tech football. "The Drought" spanned Tech's thirty-one-game unbeaten streak. It stretched through the Jackets' run of six straight bowl victories—quite an achievement at a time when bowl games were harder to qualify for than sainthood, unlike now, when there are more games than varieties of flora and fauna to name them after.

Some "Drought Makers" are among the greats of the game. Coach Bobby Dodd, guard Ray Beck, and linebackers George and Larry Morris are all in the National Football Foundation College Football Hall of Fame. Others were like Georgia's Sapp: good players who had their greatest moments in one of college football's best and bitterest rivalries. Still others were seldom-used players destined for anonymity, to be remembered only in the list of letter-winners in the school's media guide until fate touched them and turned them into heroes.

They are all "Drought Makers."

Larry Morris, an All-American and a member of the College Football Hall of Fame.

Bobby Dodd

Dodd officially became a college head coach for the first time in 1945, succeeding his longtime mentor William Alexander. Fortunately Tech's administration didn't hold his 34–0 loss to Georgia in 1942 as an interim coach against him. Dodd coached the Jackets for the final four regular-season games of 1942. Alexander was ill, and doctors ordered him to take some time off from football. Alexander suffered a heart attack the week of the Georgia game, leaving Dodd to coach undefeated Tech against 9–1 Georgia, with the winner advancing to the Rose Bowl to play for a national championship.

Georgia outmanned Tech in the game. The Jackets were without injured freshman phenom Clint Castleberry, while the Bulldogs' offense featured both Sinkwich and Trippi. The Bulldogs won in a rout. "It was a terrible defeat for us," said Bill Healy, a freshman on that Georgia Tech team. "We were unbeaten, and they had gotten beaten the week before."

The loss reinforced Dodd's belief in the overwhelming importance of the game. Losses to the Dogs in 1945, 1946, and 1948—three of his first four years after succeeding Alexander—and the criticism afterward ate at him. He once told assistant coach Frank Broyles, who would go on to become a legendary coach at Arkansas, that Tech would "have it made if there was no Georgia."

His first Georgia game as head coach went much the same way his debut against the Bulldogs as interim coach did. Georgia's Trippi threw three touchdowns and ran another as the Bull-

Breaking "the Drought"

Theron Sapp should never have had an opportunity to end "the Drought," Georgia's eight-year losing streak against Georgia Tech. He shouldn't have been on the football field. Sapp had cracked three vertebrae in his neck during a practice for a high school all-star game. He had just completed his senior season at Dublin (Georgia) High School and had chosen Georgia over several other schools.

His doctor had told him his football career ended with the injury. The vertebrae would heal but would be more susceptible to injury in the future. The wrong hit could kill him. Georgia coach Wally Butts assured Sapp the school would honor its scholarship offer, and Sapp attended classes his freshman year in a cast that covered most of his torso.

After the cast came off, Sapp wanted to play football. He convinced Butts to let him play and spent his sophomore year on the junior varsity team. He moved up to the varsity the next year.

He became a legend in his tenth game with the varsity. The game was scoreless early in the second half when Sapp hit Tech's Floyd Faucette, forcing a fumble that Sapp recovered at midfield.

A fullback on offense, Sapp carried six consecutive times on the ensuing drive to move Georgia to Tech's 1 yard line. The Bulldogs failed on a quarterback sneak on the next play, leaving them with fourth down from the 1.

Sapp got the call and plowed in for the score. Georgia held on for the victory. "The Drought" was finally over. Georgia Tech coach Bobby Dodd later summed up what Sapp's performance meant, putting it in context with the 1980 team's winning the national championship behind tailback Herschel Walker.

"Walker won the national championship for Georgia and was awarded the Heisman Trophy, but to older Bulldogs who suffered through the 1950s, Sapp's breaking the drought was greater," Dodd said. "He silenced eight years of bragging from Tech students and alumni. Breaking the Drought was a remarkable achievement."

dogs blew out Tech 33–0 before a standing-room-only crowd of 34,000 at Grant Field. The stadium held only 32,000 then.

"My boys looked better in practice Wednesday, but they still were not sharp," Dodd told reporters before the game. "They are simply burned out, but we are trying to reach the heights one more time."

Dodd's team finally reached the summit of the Georgia mountain two years later, beating the Bulldogs 7–0. The victory earned the Jackets an Orange Bowl berth, and they beat Kansas 20–14. The positive reaction in the community led Dodd to later outline his keys to keeping fans happy.

"Anytime you beat Georgia and win a bowl game, you had a great season," Dodd said. "Don't make a difference what you did against Tennessee or Kentucky or Duke. They forget those things. They remember the Georgia game and that bowl game. That was big stuff."

Bigger stuff was ahead for Dodd in the Georgia series. Take away the 1943 and 1944 seasons, when the World War II draft left the Bulldogs short-handed, and the rivals from Athens had dominated Tech for the decade. Then came the 1949 game. The first act of "the Drought."

"That's a big game," Dodd told his biographer in the book *Dodd's Luck*. "The two teams were pretty evenly matched, and it was the first of my eight years that I dominated Georgia. I needed those eight years because a lot of times, I couldn't dominate Georgia. They were tough, boy, let me tell you."

Many Jackets would make big plays during the eight games of "the Drought." But it was Dodd who gave Tech a 7–6 victory in the inaugural meeting, calling for a quick kick on a third

Coach Bobby Dodd with quarterback Darrell Crawford.

down late in the game. The Jackets trailed 6–0. Georgia scored on a long pass in the second quarter, but placekicker Bob Durant shanked the extra point. Two quarters later Tech's defense stopped the Bulldogs on fourth down and took possession at its own 34 yard line. Dodd's team made only 4 yards on its first two plays, and Georgia lined up to stuff Tech on the third-down play.

Dodd responded by calling the quick kick, which was downed at the 5 yard line. Georgia couldn't move the ball off the goal line and punted back to the Jackets, giving them the ball at the Georgia 39 yard line. Six plays later quarterback Jim Southard scored on a 1-yard sneak, and Tech won 7–6.

Dodd would make other great coaching calls over the next seven games against Georgia, including one that led to arguably the greatest play in Tech history. But it was the 1949 quick kick that kick-started "the Drought."

Lamar Wheat

Talk to any player who took part in Georgia Tech's renaissance season of 1951. To a man, they'll credit senior Lamar Wheat. "We were young, and we were hungry," said George Morris, a player Dodd called the best he ever coached. "He was a veteran and our leader. He was a dedicated football player."

Wheat also had what defensive coaches call "a nose for the football"—an uncanny ability to force and recover fumbles. So it surprised no one that when the 1950 game against Georgia was decided by a fumble, Wheat was the man on top of the football.

The Bulldogs were driving inside Tech's 20 yard line early in a scoreless game when quarterback Mal Cook called his own number on a keeper play. He took the snap and looked for running room. He bobbled the ball in the process, and Wheat, the Jackets' right tackle, dove on it at the 26 yard line.

The fumble recovery gave Georgia Tech the momentum. The offense mounted a long drive, moving down to the Georgia 21 yard line. On first down a Georgia player clobbered Tech quarterback Joe Salome and drew a roughing-the-passer penalty, giving the Jackets a first down at the Georgia 6 yard line. Darrell Crawford scored a touchdown two plays later, and Georgia Tech held on for a 7–0 victory.

Wheat would earn All-America honors the next year and captain the undefeated and Southeastern Conference champion Yellow Jackets. But he'll always be remembered for recovering that fumble.

George Maloof

Georgia Tech made rivalry history by beating the Bulldogs 48–6 in the 1951 game. The margin of victory is still Tech's largest in the series history. George Maloof scored 24 of those points all by himself.

Maloof was the fullback in Tech's "belly series" offense, a forerunner of the triple-option offense that Dodd had picked up on while serving as an assistant coach for a college all-star team in 1950. Dodd loved the offense. As an All-America quarterback at Tennessee in the late 1920s and early 1930s, Dodd was an adept ballhandler who used fakes to deceive defenders.

Misdirection and deception were the premises of the belly series. Dodd hired Frank Broyles, a great Tech quarterback in the 1940s, as his offensive coordinator before the 1951 season. The coach charged Broyles with implementing the offense. Maloof's role was to pound the middle. Quarterback Darrell Crawford handed Maloof the football or faked the handoff to him on every play, and every play Maloof plowed into the line. He was a vital piece of an offense that Dodd said "had speed galore." Against Georgia, though, he became a star. His four touchdowns, all on short dives at the goal line, remain tied for the most in a single game in Tech history.

The 1951 game also made a goat out of the Bulldogs' Zeke Bratkowski, who would go on to become an All-American and have a seventeen-year professional career. He threw eight interceptions in the blowout loss, a school record to this day. Bratkowski's last interception was returned for a 55-yard touchdown.

Bratkowski's follies are perhaps the best-remembered part of the blowout. But Maloof's touchdowns—which came just six games after wide receiver Buck Martin caught four scoring passes in a win against Auburn—will never be forgotten by Tech fans. The Georgia win earned Tech a bowl berth, its first since 1947. The Yellow Jackets defeated Baylor 17–14 in the Orange Bowl. Maloof made a key play in that victory, catching a screen pass and running 35 yards to set up a touchdown.

Chappell Rhino

The name "Rhino" is as familiar to Georgia Tech football fans as the names "Heisman," "Alexander," and "Dodd." Three generations of the Rhino family played on the Flats, including All-American Randy Rhino during the early 1970s. But Randy's dad, Chappell, is probably the most famous of the four Rhinos— Randy's brother Daniel and Randy's son Kelley are the others— because of one legendary play. Five years before Sapp earned his nickname in the rivalry, Chappell became known as "One-Play Rhino" for throwing a running pass in Tech's 23–9 victory.

Rhino was a senior reserve on the 1952 team. He was a star baseball player for the Yellow Jackets, playing infield and outfield and pitching. On the football field, though, he was a seldom-used defensive back. His date with immortality would come in the next-to-last game of his football career. Georgia Tech came into the 1952 game the owner of a twenty-four-game unbeaten streak. Tech was on the brink of its second consecutive unbeaten season, and a win against Georgia would give the Jackets a chance to play for a national championship.

Tech's players felt like the steam whistle that sits at the center of the Atlanta campus. Every weekday during classes, at five minutes to the hour, the whistle blows to signal the end of a class period. Tech's players were under similar pressure. And on the first play from scrimmage, quarterback Bill Brigman blew. He fumbled the ball. Georgia recovered and scored to go ahead 7–0. "They weren't having a good year, but our halfback Leon Hardeman was hurt and didn't play," George Morris said. "It was going to be close."

Chappell Rhino (with ball) threw the most famous pass in Georgia Tech football history.

The Yellow Jackets cut the deficit to 7–3 before halftime on a Pepper Rodgers field goal. The Jacket offense fed off the late field goal, coming out early in the second half with a good drive. Georgia Tech started on its own 33 yard line and moved to Georgia's 10 yard line. Georgia Tech faced fourth down with 4 yards to go when Dodd called upstairs to Broyles in the coaches' booth and recommended a running pass. Tech practiced the play nearly every day and used it regularly in games.

But never had Dodd put Rhino in to throw the pass. Broyles couldn't recall Rhino ever even trying it in practice. But Dodd said it had to be Rhino. "I thought Chappell was enough of an athlete to where he could do it for me," Dodd said in his biography. "And I didn't think he'd choke up on me, and he didn't."

Rhino took the toss from Brigman and ran to his right. Georgia's cornerback bit. He broke off coverage of Tech receiver Buck Martin and went after Rhino. Rhino then earned his nickname, tossing the ball to a wide-open Martin for the touchdown that gave his team a 10–7 lead.

The play was like a long, hard pull on the chain of the steam whistle. It released all the pressure on the Yellow Jackets. Bobby Moorhead would later intercept a Bratkowski pass and return it to the Georgia 1 yard line, setting up the clinching touchdown. Tech added another score in the closing minutes for a 23–9 victory. The next day Chappell Rhino became "One-Play Rhino."

Pepper Rodgers

Of all the characters ever to play football at Georgia Tech, from "Indian" Joe Guyon in the 1910s and Stumpy Thomason in the 1920s to Kim King in the 1960s and Marco Coleman in the 1990s, Pepper Rodgers may be the most colorful. The day before his first college game in 1951, Rodgers told Dodd he'd never miss if named the starting placekicker. He made good on the pledge, hitting several game-winning field goals in his career, including

Pepper Rodgers (center, calling a play) starred as both a placekicker and a quarterback during his Georgia Tech playing days.

the first ever to decide an Orange Bowl. Rodgers was a freshman.

Rodgers would also make his mark as a coach at Tech. He succeeded Bill Fulcher in 1974 and coached the Jackets to six solid yet unspectacular seasons. At the height of the disco era, Rodgers rode a motorcycle to work, wore a perm in his hair, and incorporated aerobics into daily practices.

Rodgers the quarterback is what rivalry followers remember most. He threw for one touchdown and ran for another in a

28–12 Tech victory in 1953, stretching "the Drought" to five years. Georgia was wrapping up its worst season since 1932 when it visited Grant Field on November 28, 1953. Rodgers, a senior, had witnessed two previous victories over Georgia. He expected a third. "I thought we had better players than they did in those years," Rodgers said. "And we had a strategic-wise coach in coach Dodd. We were supposed to beat those guys."

The Yellow Jackets' talent advantage showed. They led 14–0 at the end of the first quarter. But the Bulldogs answered with a touchdown and were driving to tie the game. Georgia's Bratkowski completed a long pass down the sideline to wide-open receiver Charlie Madison. He inexplicably fumbled—no Tech player was near him—at the 5 yard line, though, and the Jackets' Ben Dougherty recovered.

The turnover swung the momentum back to Georgia Tech. Rodgers led them down the field, and halfback Billy Teas threw his only pass of the season, a 12-yard touchdown toss that put Tech in front 21–6. Rodgers added a touchdown pass late in the victory.

The win against Georgia earned the Yellow Jackets a Sugar Bowl berth against West Virginia. Rodgers capped his career by accounting for 23 points in the 42–19 victory, throwing three touchdown passes and kicking a field goal and 2 extra points.

Wade Mitchell

Wade Mitchell was three times a hero against Georgia. He threw the game-winning touchdown pass in a 7–3 victory in 1954, made a touchdown-saving and momentum-swinging tackle in the 21–3 win in 1955, and ran for a score in a 35–0 blowout in 1956.

Mitchell's standout career against Georgia started with a thud, though. Mitchell shared time with Rodgers at quarterback in 1953. Just a freshman, he was a strong runner and provided a good change of pace from Rodgers. He got into the Georgia game early in the second quarter with Tech ahead 14–0. But he fumbled at the Jacket 25 yard line, setting up a Bulldog touchdown.

Georgia Tech recovered from his gaffe, of course, and Rodgers led them to the victory. And Mitchell took advantage of all three chances at redemption. He didn't exactly star the next year. Rain fell at Sanford Stadium starting twelve hours before kickoff and continued throughout the game. On Tech's first possession Mitchell fumbled again. Georgia recovered, and the miscue led to a Bulldog field goal—their first ever against Tech. Mitchell couldn't move the Yellow Jacket offense the rest of the first half. They went without a first down and trailed 3–0 at halftime.

The rain worsened during the break, turning the field into a quagmire. Tech kicked off to Georgia to start the second half. On the Bulldogs' first play Jimmy Harper fumbled the ball away at his team's 19 yard line. Mitchell seized his chance. He threw a touchdown pass to Henry Hair on the next play. It would be his only completion of the day, but it was enough for a 7–3 Tech victory.

Mitchell made a big play early the next year. Georgia's Bobby Garrard broke free on his team's first possession. He lost his shoe during the run, though, and Mitchell, who played defensive back as well as quarterback, caught and tackled Garrard at the 12 yard line. Georgia had to settle for a field goal, its only points of the game. Mitchell added a touchdown run later in the 21–3 victory.

Mitchell ignited the blowout in 1956 in his final game

against the Bulldogs. Tech led 7–0 at halftime before Mitchell moved his team 72 yards for a touchdown on the opening drive of the second half. Mitchell capped the march with a 1-yard run, and Tech piled up the points from there. Mitchell made the All-SEC team his senior season. He was later enshrined in the Georgia Tech Athletic Hall of Fame, where he is remembered fondly—particularly for his play against Georgia.

"The Drought" marked a turning point in both Georgia Tech and Georgia's programs, best summed up as the rise of Dodd and the decline of Wally Butts. Dodd departed from the old southern football axiom of grind-it-out offense, relying instead on small and quick players, while Butts stuck with the style that made him so successful in winning two national championships in the 1940s.

"It wasn't that Georgia didn't have a talented team, they just played a game in the trenches," said Don Ellis, who played end for Tech from 1954 to 1956. "We beat those kinds of teams all the time."

Sapp would end Georgia's misery in 1957, the first of four straight Bulldog wins in the series. Dodd would reestablish Tech's dominance by winning in 1961, Butts's last season, and again in 1962 and 1963. The next year Vince Dooley took over Georgia's program and did to Dodd what Dodd had done to Butts. Dooley won his first five games against the Yellow Jackets, helping drive Dodd out of coaching following the 1966 season.

But "the Drought" and its makers will never be forgotten.

Quarterback Wade Mitchell led Georgia Tech to three wins during "the Drought."

The "Greatest Victory" Ever

The day dawned dark and rainy. To Alabama football coach Paul "Bear" Bryant, it was as if his rival, Georgia Tech coach Bobby Dodd, had struck a secret deal with Mother Nature. Or with someone even more sinister. A secret deal would explain much about Dodd and his so-called luck. Proof of such a deal would put many of his peers at ease. They explained away many failures against Georgia Tech as just another case of "Dodd's luck," but in the end, they were left with self-doubt.

Bryant was already steeling himself for those haunting thoughts on the morning of November 17, 1962. He stared blankly toward Grant Field from the window of his suite at the Georgian Terrace Hotel. Nothing could brighten his mood. Not even a visit from a promising high school quarterback, one who accepted Bryant's invitation despite a strong relationship with Georgia Tech and Dodd.

Kim King, his parents, and his girlfriend walked into the suite and found Bryant slumped in a chair by the window. A pack of cigarettes rested on each armrest, Chesterfields on one side, Benson and Hedges on the other. "This is Dodd's weather. This is Dodd's kind of weather," Bryant told the Kings in between drags on his cigarette.

Bryant's torment puzzled the Kings. Alabama was defending national champion and ranked number one in the country. Joe Namath quarterbacked the team. "Coach Bryant, you've got a national championship team. You've got all these players back," Kim King's father told the coach.

Bryant remained dour. "It's raining. It's a sloppy field. This is Dodd's weather. This is Dodd's weather. He'll figure out how to play in this weather. He knows how to win in this kind of weather," Bryant said.

The memory of the scene was one of King's favorite anecdotes. He told it often prior to his death in 2004. He recounted the conversation in his autobiography, *Kim King's Tales from the Georgia Tech Sideline.*

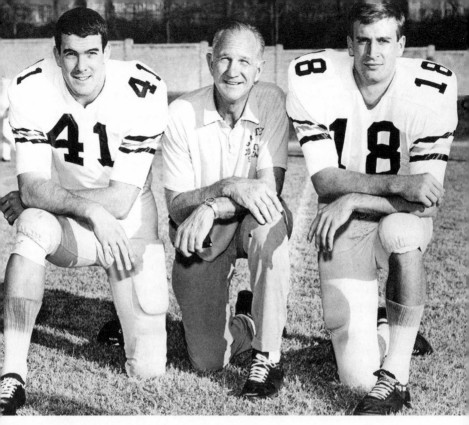

Bobby Dodd (center) with Lenny Snow (left) and Kim King in 1966.

Bryant proved prophetic that morning. Dodd's Georgia Tech team slopped its way to a 7–6 victory over the Crimson Tide later that day, ending Bama's twenty-six-game winning streak. Dodd summed up the game simply, calling it his "greatest victory" ever. It was also one of the last games between two coaches who were as much friends as rivals. The two shared an immeasurable amount of respect. In fact, both joked that if they could co-coach a team—Bryant at practice during the week and Dodd on game day—they'd never lose.

Yet the 1962 game marked the start of a new era in the Dodd-Bryant relationship—a dark one. An incident in the previous year's game had strained their friendship. Alabama won the game 10–0, its fourth straight victory in the series.

Being shut out by the Tide didn't bother Dodd nearly as much as one of his players being the target of a cheap shot by one of Bryant's players and Bryant's subsequent comments about the situation. Alabama linebacker Darwin Holt was one of those infamous players whose antics today would make him an urban legend. He played to the whistle and often beyond its blowing. He was the type you never wanted to be next to on the bottom of a pileup for fear he'd bite you.

Holt was also a player an opponent should never take his eyes off of, as Georgia Tech's Chick Graning learned in the 1961 game. Graning captained the Yellow Jackets that season, playing halfback on offense and linebacker on defense. He played on Georgia Tech's punt teams as well. That's how he met Holt. Tech punted to Alabama in the fourth quarter of the game at Legion Field in Birmingham. Tide returner Billy Richardson called for a fair catch and fielded the kick.

Graning stood upfield, guarding the sideline against a return. After Richardson caught the punt, Graning relaxed. But before Graning could return to the defensive huddle for the next series, Holt slammed into him, thrusting his elbow under Graning's face mask and knocking him unconscious. Holt didn't even look back until reaching Alabama's sideline.

Holt's elbow fractured several of Graning's facial bones, knocked out five teeth, broke his nose, fractured his sinuses, and left him with a concussion. The cheap shot was not unlike the infamous one Kermit Washington dealt Rudy Tomjanovich during an NBA game sixteen years later.

Georgia Tech's team doctor, Lamont Henry, later called it "the worst facial injury I have ever seen in my twenty years of association with athletics." Dodd declined comment on the altercation following the game, choosing to address it privately. In his biography, *Dodd's Luck*, Georgia Tech's coach said he called Bryant the day after the game and demanded Holt be punished. Bryant refused.

The officials didn't penalize Holt—the incident was so far away from the play none of them saw it—so Bryant chose not to punish his player. Dodd then turned to the media. The coach showed the game film on his weekly TV show, and Atlanta newspaper columnists responded with the outrage that Bryant failed to show. Furman Bisher penned several columns on Holt's cheap shot and Bryant's reaction, comparing their actions with a form of Charles Darwin's theory of evolution—survival of the fittest.

Holt later visited Graning to apologize personally. But the incident ended the Georgia Tech senior's playing career. And the situation and its aftermath may have led to the discontinuation of the series between the two schools three years later. Dodd denied that assertion in *Dodd's Luck*, saying he quit playing Bryant following the 1964 season because he was tired of losing to him. Bryant's Alabama teams went 6–1 against Dodd's Tech teams.

Georgia Tech's departure from the Southeastern Conference in 1964 made the series' discontinuation that much easier. The 1962 game remains a classic. Bryant opened his postgame press conference by saying, "We saw one of the greatest football games I have ever seen. It was a great, great game. It was certainly a great victory for Tech."

Bye-Bye, SEC

Georgia Tech helped form the Southeastern Conference in 1933, becoming a charter member. Thirty years later the school became one of the first to leave the league. Dodd pulled Tech out of the SEC following the 1963–64 academic year because of the conference's "140 rule." League schools were allowed to put 140 football and basketball players on scholarship at the time. With fewer than fifteen basketball players on scholarship at most schools, the football team could carry 125 to 130 scholarship players—more than that, actually, because the league didn't check the numbers until after football season.

Although those numbers far exceed the current limit of eighty-five scholarship players, the rule put Dodd in a bind. He recruited more than thirty players each year, and many of them stayed on scholarship for five years. And unlike many other coaches in the conference, Dodd refused to run off unwanted players during the regular season to meet the standards of the "140 rule."

In his biography, *Dodd's Luck,* the coach said the situation amounted to a "legal tryout" of players at the other schools. Dodd worked to change the rule. He convinced coaches and officials at five other SEC schools to vote with him to overturn the rule at the 1964 conference meetings. The swing vote belonged to Alabama. Dodd lobbied his friend, Paul "Bear" Bryant, to recommend a vote to change the rule to his president.

Bryant agreed to try, but Alabama's president felt differently. He cast the first vote in the meeting and showed his support for the rule. Edwin Harrison, Tech's president, immediately announced his school's withdrawal from the SEC. Tech competed as an independent for the next fifteen years. The Yellow Jackets joined the Atlantic Coast Conference in 1979.

The game proved that pretty is not a prerequisite for great. The Yellow Jackets totaled just 126 yards. Quarterback Billy Lothridge finished with 53 yards total offense—including 4 yards rushing—on seventeen carries.

Alabama's two quarterbacks, Namath and Jack Hurlbut, combined to complete only fourteen of twenty-eight passes and threw four interceptions. Namath was the Tide's leading rusher with 32 yards. Stat sheets make for poor storytellers, though. Drama is best built gradually, even slowly. And the 52,971 fans in attendance never lost the buzz they arrived at Grant Field with that afternoon.

The game had sold out months earlier. Season passes cost $33 in 1962 and were gobbled up immediately after going on sale in June. Single-game tickets went for $5.50 each, and two games quickly sold out: Tennessee and Alabama. Tech had gone 7–4 and appeared in the Gator Bowl the previous year, ending a four-year run of seasons in which Dodd's teams won fewer than seven games.

Expectations were high for the 1962 team as a result. Georgia Tech opened with lopsided victories over Clemson and Florida and rose to number five in the national rankings. But the Jackets lost to Louisiana State 10–7 when the Tigers returned the second-half kickoff for a touchdown. The defeat dropped Georgia Tech out of the top ten. The Jackets redeemed themselves with fans the next week, shutting out Tennessee.

Auburn spoiled Tech's 3–1 start on October 20, though, upsetting the Yellow Jackets 17–14 on a blustery day at Birmingham's Legion Field. Going into the 22-mph winds early in the game, the Jackets fell behind 17–0. A second-half rally fell short. The Jackets rebounded from the Auburn loss by defeating Tulane and Duke and tying Florida State. Georgia Tech headed into the

Alabama game with a record of 5–2–1. The annual grudge match with Georgia followed the Alabama game, but Tech had an open date the following week before meeting the Bulldogs. The Jackets' focus was squarely on the Crimson Tide.

The game opened methodically. In the grand tradition of southern football, the two teams felt each other out in the opening minutes. Georgia Tech mounted its first threat on its third possession. Dodd turned Lothridge loose, calling three straight pass plays to open the drive. The junior quarterback completed all three as the Jackets moved down to the Alabama 16 yard line.

Lothridge made few mistakes that season. He led the Southeastern Conference in total offense with 1,484 yards. He gained nearly a third of those yards running the ball and was the SEC's second-leading rusher despite his well-publicized lack of speed. Lothridge countered his athletic shortcomings with a sharp football mind. Dodd said in his biography that Lothridge reminded him much of himself as a player. Lothridge could kick, pass, and run just like Dodd and thought through the game much the same way the coach had during his All-America career at Tennessee.

Dodd thought so much of Lothridge that he took unusual steps to ensure Lothridge would come to Tech. The night before signing day, the coach invited Lothridge and the quarterback's high school teammate, Billy Martin, to his house to shoot pool. The maneuver kept other coaches from making last-minute recruiting pushes. And minutes after midnight, Dodd signed both players to letters of intent.

Lothridge became the starting quarterback at the start of the 1962 season and played almost flawlessly all year. He made a huge error on that first long drive against Alabama, though. The passing success of the previous three plays convinced Dodd and Lothridge to continue throwing the ball. On a first-down play from Bama's 16 yard line, Lothridge threw an interception, the first of two Tech turnovers in the game.

Perhaps Bryant saw the turnover as an omen, because minutes later he decided to go for it on fourth down. The play failed, and Tech took over at the Alabama 48 yard line. After the game Bryant said the call "handicapped" his team. Even so, Georgia Tech failed to capitalize on the miscue and the resulting good field position. Lothridge moved the ball inside the 30 yard line before the drive stalled, and Lothridge missed a 43-yard field goal. The first quarter ended in a scoreless tie.

The legend of Mike McNames was born minutes later. McNames came to Georgia Tech in 1959, an undersize halfback straight out of the sweet onion fields of Vidalia, Georgia. He walked onto the team as a freshman and earned a scholarship. By the end of his junior season, he was the Jackets' leading rusher as well as a gritty defender. The substitution rules of the day still forced teams to play Iron Man football.

McNames fit the Iron Man mold perfectly. Despite his size—5'10", 196 pounds—he was a sure tackler with good hands. Early in the second quarter against Alabama, he made two of the biggest plays of his career. Georgia Tech's defensive line rattled Namath early in the game. He had yet to become "Broadway Joe," issue Super Bowl guarantees, and don furs on the sideline or nylons in advertisements. He was considered one of the nation's top quarterbacks, though. And after Alabama struggled moving the ball in the first quarter against Tech, Namath looked to pass the Tide down the field in the second quarter.

Alabama faced second-and-10 at its own 28 yard line when Namath dropped back to throw. Tech's Martin—Lothridge's high school teammate who had shot pool with Dodd the night before signing day—hit Namath just as he released a pass downfield. McNames picked off the throw, just his third interception of the season. Two plays later he ran for a 9-yard touchdown. Lothridge's extra point made it 7–0. Georgia Tech took its touchdown lead into halftime. Tech outgained Alabama 108 yards to 75 in the first half, and Namath was three of nine passing for 31 yards with an interception. "Tech was well prepared for us mentally and physically," Bryant said.

And after Dodd had a lead, it was hard for even a Bryant-coached team to wrestle it away. Alabama got the ball first to start the second half and went three plays and out. Dodd turned to one of his favorite strategies on the ensuing possession—Tech quick-kicked on third down, content to try to make Alabama play the last two quarters on its own end of the field.

The Tide took possession at their own 5 yard line. But instead of playing conservatively with his back to the goal line, Namath ran and passed his team out to midfield. The drive stalled, but Alabama's special teams downed a punt at Georgia Tech's 1 yard line. Dodd's strategy had backfired. It appeared the second half would be played in Georgia Tech territory.

But along came McNames again. He picked off Namath a second time in the opening minute of the fourth quarter and returned the interception to midfield. Dodd didn't hesitate—he quick-kicked again, pushing Alabama back inside its own 20 yard line. The Tide picked up a first down on the ensuing possession before Bryant countered with his own quick kick. The punt pinned Tech back at its own 15 yard line. Four plays later the game took an awkward turn. Actually an awkward snap.

Georgia Tech faced fourth-and-2 from its own 23 yard line. Lothridge lined up to punt. The snap came low, though, and in scooping up the ball and kicking it away, Lothridge touched his knee down at the 9 yard line. Alabama ball, first-and-goal, with 7:16 left. Bama needed four plays and a controversial Tech penalty to score and pull within a point of Tech at 7–6. The touchdown forced Bryant to make a difficult decision. If he kicked the extra point, the game would likely end in a tie. In an era before overtime and the Bowl Championship Series, a tie was as damaging as a loss for a team trying to win a national championship. Bryant decided to go for two. "I had no hesitation at all" in making the call, Bryant said after the game.

The conversion failed. Hurlbut, in at quarterback, tried a sneak. Tech's McNames—who else?—and Jeff Davis, who finished the game with twelve tackles, stopped Hurlbut short of the goal line. The Yellow Jacket players responded as if they'd just won the game and were flagged for a celebration penalty as a result. Kicking off near midfield, Alabama tried an onside kick. It worked. Nelson Elmore recovered at Tech's 33 yard line. So much for "Dodd's luck."

The next five minutes were excruciating for fans of both teams. Namath was more Joe fool than Joe cool, throwing his third interception on the first play after the successful onside kick. Frank Sexton picked off the pass for Georgia Tech. A lanky junior from Knoxville, Tennessee, he caught the ball and turned upfield to try for a long return. That's when an Alabama player hit him and forced a fumble.

Coach Bobby Dodd celebrates the 1962 upset of Alabama, a win he called his "greatest victory."

The Crimson Tide recovered. They had one more chance to pull out the victory and extend their winning streak. Bryant kept the ball on the ground the first several plays of the next drive. Namath broke free on a 15-yard run for a first down at the Tech 13 yard line.

Maybe the run took something out of Namath. Or maybe Bryant feared his star quarterback would throw another interception. The reasoning aside, Hurlbut lined up at quarterback instead of Namath on the first-down play—and proceeded to throw a pass right to Georgia Tech's Don Toner. Toner was one of the few Yellow Jackets who didn't play both ways. Dodd described the 5'8", 174-pound safety as the "Jackets' surest tackler in the open field" in the team's publicity guide. An injury cut short his 1961 season, but Toner recovered in time to play his entire senior year. And in one of his last games, he made the biggest play. "Our pass defense had its best day of the season against the best throwers we have faced," Dodd said in the postgame press conference.

Bryant, meanwhile, lamented the pass call. "If I had it to do over again, I would run two quarterback sneaks and kick" a field goal, the Bear said. Georgia Tech and its fans celebrated the victory for much of the next week. Dodd called it the greatest single victory ever won by a Georgia Tech football team in bowl games or the regular season. The momentum carried over to the season finale against Georgia: Tech hammered the rival 37–6.

Alabama did likewise to its nemesis, Auburn, the following week. The Crimson Tide won 38–0 and finished with a 9–1 record. The Tech loss cost the Tide back-to-back national titles, though. They finished with a number five ranking in the final polls.

The Yellow Jackets finished the 1962 season unranked. But for one afternoon at least, they played like the nation's best.

The Passless Upset

Notre Dame's defenders danced and gyrated. They jumped on each other and whacked on one another's helmets. It seemed as if they'd just won a national championship, not sacked Georgia Tech quarterback Gary Lanier on the second play of a regular-season game. Lanier got the sack celebration's message, though: If you're going to drop back to pass against this defense, it's going to be a long afternoon. The Fighting Irish came to Atlanta on November 6, 1976, ranked number eleven in the country. Defensive tackle Bob Golic, who would go on to a Pro Bowl NFL career, anchored one of the nation's top defenses, and the Irish were heavy favorites against a Georgia Tech team with a 3–4–1 record and a true freshman playing at quarterback.

Lanier rose to his feet slowly after the sack. He wasn't hurt. He just needed some time to figure out what happened. One second he was carrying out a play-action fake, the next second Notre Dame's Ross Browner was on his back, driving him to the turf.

Then came the sack dance. As Browner celebrated, an audible groan escaped from the capacity crowd of 50,079 at Grant Field. Yellow Jacket coach Pepper Rodgers sighed too and signaled for a time-out. As Lanier came off the field, Rodgers turned to his offensive assistant coaches. "That's the last time they strut on Grant Field," Rodgers told them. "They're going to have to squat and stop the option from now on. I'm not calling another pass play."

Lanier made it to the sideline in time to hear the end of the conversation. "Coach, I don't have a problem with that. That's fine with me," he told Rodgers.

Thirty years later coach and quarterback still recall the conversation the same way. Lanier has had his share of practice in telling the story: He's asked about the Notre Dame game dozens of times a year. At football and basketball games. At Georgia Tech club meetings. On the street.

The game made him a pseudo-celebrity and gave him an athlete's most coveted gift: a claim to fame. Gary Lanier is the quarterback who beat Notre Dame without throwing a pass.

"It's ironic that you can be remembered for something like that," Lanier said. "You'd think the quarterback would be the last player to be remembered for a game like that."

Lanier is a part of Georgia Tech lore instead. He became a forgotten player later in his career, losing the starting job his junior season when the Jackets switched from the triple-option offense to an I-formation set. But Tech followers will always recall the day he ran and pitched the Yellow Jackets to a 23–14 upset of the Fighting Irish. "Maybe it was just our day," Lanier said. "Everything we did seemed to work. As for not throwing a pass, those who saw me throw a ball understood why we didn't pass."

Lanier lacked passing prowess. He had the arm and height of a second baseman, not exactly a good combination for a major college quarterback. He stood 5'9" with his cleats on and his time in the 40-yard dash never caused a timekeeper to do a double-take. He was so inept as a passer that he worked with the flankers, not the quarterbacks, during individual drills at Georgia Tech practices. Those physical limitations almost kept him from playing at Tech. How he ended up under center in the game against Notre Dame is a tale even more amazing than the story of what transpired that afternoon.

Lanier grew up a Yellow Jacket fan in Savannah, Georgia, listening to Al Ciraldo call games on the radio. His father was a big Tech fan, drawn to the Jackets by the Bobby Dodd teams of the 1950s. Lanier dreamed of playing for Georgia Tech. And when Rodgers brought the triple-option to the Flats in 1974, it seemed like destiny to Lanier. He possessed quick feet, and he was raised on the option. He starred at Benedictine Military School, a high school football factory of the day, and attracted the attention of option coaches. Bobby Ross, then coach of the Citadel in Charleston, South Carolina, recruited Lanier. So did coaches at small schools such as Presbyterian and Newberry.

Rodgers and his staff also kept up with Lanier. He auditioned for Tech at a summer camp before his senior year at Benedictine. He received a letter from the Yellow Jacket coaches that September. "It said they felt at that time I wasn't fast enough or big enough to play," Lanier said. "They invited me to come as a walk-on."

Disappointed, Lanier spent the rest of his senior season trying to prove he was good enough to play at Georgia Tech. He didn't want to play small college football, and although he respected the Citadel's Ross, the idea of spending four more years at a military school didn't appeal to him. He ended up having a "pretty good season" at Benedictine and received another letter from Georgia Tech over the holidays.

This note invited him for a campus visit. He left Atlanta that weekend with a scholarship offer. "I couldn't wait to get home and tell my parents, it was such a big thrill," Lanier said. "It was pretty late in the process, and it was probably a case where they had a scholarship left over and figured they'd offer it to me. But I didn't care why they offered it."

Rodgers brought Lanier in because of his option experience. Benedictine's offense was almost identical to Rodgers's, right down to the footwork and the way the quarterback carried out his fakes. Lanier also had deft touch in pitching the ball to his back on the option. "He wasn't as good as some of the other option quarterbacks I had, but he could pitch the ball as well as anybody I've ever seen," the coach said.

Rodgers and Lanier often joked about the quarterback's skills. Lanier would come in the day after a game and tell Rodgers, "Coach, I've been watching TV, and a forward pass there is when you throw it down the field." Rodgers always had the same response: "No, a forward pass for you, Lanier, is a pitch backwards. That's your best pass."

Lanier arrived at Georgia Tech in August of 1976 figuring the only passes—forward or backward—he'd throw that fall would be in practice. His goal? Make the travel squad. Maybe earn a letter. He ended up doing much more. Rodgers opened camp without a starting quarterback. Danny Myers, the starter during Rodgers's first two years at Tech, had graduated. The coach intentionally loaded his roster with quarterbacks and spent the preseason evaluating them. He moved the speediest ones to the defensive secondary before the season started. He kept four others, including Lanier, at quarterback.

One drawback to the triple-option offense is the risk of quarterback injury. He is hit much more often than a pocket passer and usually on the move, where knees and ankles are exposed to tacklers. By the fourth game of the 1976 season, Georgia Tech had lost two quarterbacks to injury. Mike Jolly was the starter, Lanier his backup.

The Yellow Jackets played host to Virginia on October 2, 1976. Tech was winless, but Jolly had led them to a tie with Clemson the week before. He carried that momentum over against the Cavaliers, staking the Jackets to an early lead.

Early in the second quarter, though, a defender rolled up on Jolly's ankle. The injury would end not just his season but also his career. As Jolly was helped from the field, Rodgers looked at Lanier and took a deep breath. "It was like he was saying to himself, 'Either put in Lanier or fold,'" Lanier said. "So he put me in. I didn't have a whole lot of time to think about it, or I probably would have gotten really nervous."

The Day Pepper's Perm Died

Pepper Rodgers is without question the most colorful coach in Georgia Tech history and possibly in the history of college football. The brash, offensive genius came to Georgia Tech in 1974 having fully embraced the lifestyle of the day. He rode a motorcycle to the office, shunned socks, and permed his hair.

Pepper's permanent didn't sit well with many of Georgia Tech's traditional fans. "Bear Bryant didn't wear no perm," Rodgers heard from fans.

He ignored the complaints, though, until the day after Tech's 1976 upset of Notre Dame. His mother, Louise, attended the 23–14 victory, and as she filed out of Grant Field among the other fans following the victory, she overheard a woman say, "That was a good win, but I still don't like Pepper's hair."

Louise Rodgers jumped to her son's defense. "Maybe he doesn't like your hair."

The woman answered, "Who are you?"

"Well, I'm his aunt," Louise answered uncomfortably.

Rodgers couldn't believe it—his own mother wouldn't claim him. "That was the demise of my permanent," Rodgers said. "I cut my hair the next day."

Although it is covered with his cap here, Pepper Rodgers wore a permanent in his hair while serving as Georgia Tech's head coach.

Lanier made good on the battlefield promotion. He leaned heavily on his experience at Benedictine. Virginia's defense focused on taking away the fullback dive, and the defensive end was content to hit Lanier as he moved down the line on the option. That left backs Eddie Lee Ivery and David Sims with open running lanes, so Lanier pitched it to them again and again. "I took some shots, but it was worth it," Lanier said. Georgia Tech beat Virginia 35–14, and Lanier came away confident.

"Gary knew how to run the option," Ivery said. "He knew when to pitch it, and he was always right on the mark. You never had to slow down or break stride. You caught it and went."

Lanier was far from perfect his freshman season, though. Georgia Tech played Duke the week before Notre Dame, and Lanier went into the game with a 3–1 record as a starter. He struggled from the start, though, and when a bad pitch resulted in a turnover early in the second half of the 31–7 loss to the Blue Devils, Lanier came to the sideline ready for a tongue-lashing from his coach. Rodgers instead put his arm around his quarterback's shoulders. "Lanier, don't worry about it," Rodgers said. "It's not your fault, it's mine. I should never have had a quarterback of your abilities out there."

The pepless pep talk stunned Lanier. "That was a real vote of confidence, huh?" he said.

The Duke loss shook fans' confidence in the Yellow Jackets as well. The question wasn't whether they would lose to Notre Dame the next week, but rather by how many points. The Irish had beaten Tech 24–3 the year before in South Bend, Indiana, and the forecast was for a much more lopsided score in the rematch at Grant Field. "I don't think anybody in America thought we had a chance of beating that Notre Dame team," Ivery said. "Not even our own families."

Those in Georgia Tech's locker room believed, though. Notre Dame hadn't faced an option team all year, and preparing for the unique offense is hard to do in a week of practice, particularly late in the season when players are tired and injured. Plus, the Irish came into the game confident. Too confident.

And their arrogance grew in the first half. First came the sack of Lanier. Then they took a 14–3 lead with just under two minutes left before halftime. Rodgers and Lanier saw cracks in the Irish defense by the middle of the second quarter, though. Notre Dame was playing the option well but had become overzealous in outside pursuit.

Rodgers began to exploit the weakness following Notre Dame's second score, calling a cross-buck play. Lanier would fake the handoff on the fullback dive as usual, but instead of rolling down the line on the option, he'd quickly hand the ball to Sims or Ivery coming back the opposite direction.

The misdirection confused the Irish defenders. Just as they adjusted for the cross-buck, Rodgers called a reverse to flanker Drew Hill. The play picked up 30 yards, and a frustrated Notre Dame defensive back drew a penalty for hitting Hill out of bounds at the end of the run. The flag gave the Yellow Jackets a first down deep in Notre Dame territory, and Lanier scored a few plays later on an 8-yard run. Tech went into halftime trailing 14–10. Rodgers's halftime speech was short and simple. "See, these guys aren't any better than you guys," he told his team.

The Yellow Jacket defense already knew that to be true. The play of the defense that afternoon often gets lost in the fervor over

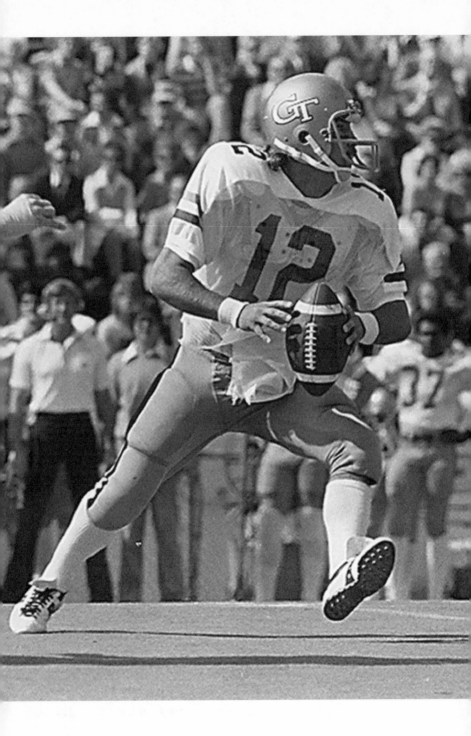

the passless offensive game plan, but it was superb. Led by line-backers Reggie Wilkes and Lucius Sanford and safety Don Bessil-lieu, the Jackets held Notre Dame to 178 yards.

The Irish couldn't move the ball. Only two plays went for longer than 10 yards. One of their two scoring drives measured just 35 yards, coming courtesy of a botched punt snap. Tech shut out Notre Dame in the second half, holding the Irish to 21 yards rushing. "Nobody remembers or talks about it, but the defense was tremendous that game," Lanier said. "It seemed like we as an offense were on the field the whole game. We'd score or punt, and they'd get the ball right back for us."

Georgia Tech's efficiency flustered the Irish. Rodgers contin-ued to mix the cross-buck into his play-calling in the second half. Sims scored on a 10-yard run to give the Jackets a 16–14 lead with 2:59 left in the third quarter. The touchdown came on another brilliant call by Rodgers—a fake play-action pass that Lanier pitched to Sims. "Pepper and his staff called a perfect game," Sims said afterward. "I mean a perfect game."

Sims extended Georgia Tech's lead to 9 points midway through the fourth quarter. He scored on a 16-yard run to make the score 23–14. Notre Dame's backup quarterback threw an interception on the ensuing possession, and Lanier ran out the clock from there.

Tech finished the game with 368 yards of offense and no turnovers. Sims led with 123 yards on fifteen carries, followed by Ivery with 81 yards on seventeen attempts. Lanier had twelve car-ries for 20 yards. The upset stunned the crowd. The game was

Gary Lanier prepares to pitch the ball to a halfback—his "best pass,"
in the opinion of coach Pepper Rodgers.

Tech's homecoming, and the alumni were overjoyed. Astute observers had noticed the Jackets had not attempted a pass in the game, and word spread quickly.

Lanier spent the rest of the day celebrating with his family and high school coach, all of whom had come up from Savannah for the game. He went to bed early, though, anxious to get up Sunday morning and read the newspaper headlines.

"I expected something like 'Lanier Leads Jackets as a Freshman,'" Lanier said. "And I couldn't wait to read these quotes by Pepper about this freshman quarterback who just beat Notre Dame. After what he said to me after the fumble against Duke, I figured he'd say something positive." Rodgers told reporters something that made Lanier laugh instead. "Of all the quarterbacks who have beaten Notre Dame, Lanier was the worst," the coach said.

"That was such a great line," Lanier said. "Pepper was so good to me. He gave me an opportunity when nobody else would. I was fortunate to be surrounded by a lot of great players that day, and I think that was the point he was really trying to make."

Rodgers admits one of his real intentions was to try to keep his freshman quarterback humble. If the coach's comments didn't do it, a 34–28 loss the next week at Navy did. Tech lost the following week as well, falling 13–10 to rival Georgia in Athens. The Jackets finished with a 4–6–1 record, their first losing season under Rodgers. "That stretch of games, from the Duke game on, we just couldn't put it all together except for against Notre Dame," Lanier said. "We had the talent. We were just on that rollercoaster. One week we had the confidence, the next week we just struggled."

The 1977 season went much the same way. Georgia Tech won four straight games in the middle of the year and was 5–2 heading into the final four weeks of the season. The Jackets lost three of their last four, though, including a rematch with Notre Dame. The lone win in that stretch was an upset of Georgia.

Eddie Lee Ivery rushed for 900 yards in 1977, averaging 5.9 yards per carry. His talents convinced Rodgers to scrap the wishbone, at least for Ivery's senior season in 1978. Ivery needed to get the ball 20 to 25 times per game, not 10 to 12 times, and that required a switch to the I-formation.

It also demanded a quarterback who could throw the ball in play-action to keep defenses from focusing too much on Ivery. Mike Kelley, a freshman from Augusta, Georgia, replaced Lanier at quarterback and threw for 1,479 yards his first season. "It was a good decision, the right decision," Lanier said. "You have a back as good as Eddie Lee, he needs to touch the ball twenty-five to thirty times."

Lanier spent his last two years as Tech's pooch punter and punt returner in fair-catch situations. He played very few snaps but dressed for every game and lettered both years. And he's still remembered well for the Notre Dame game. His own kids give him grief about it. "My son once said to me, 'Dad, it's a good thing you beat Notre Dame, because if you hadn't, no one would know who you are,'" Lanier said. "And you know what? He's right. But I don't mind that a bit."

Eddie Lee Legend

Eddie Lee Ivery had never seen snow, at least not like this. Ivery stared out the window of Georgia Tech's charter flight as it descended into Colorado Springs, mesmerized by the weather conditions. Ivery could recall every snowfall he'd ever seen in his hometown of Thomson, Georgia. The white stuff would dust the farm fields and the ditches along the roads before blowing away or melting.

What Ivery saw out the airplane window on the morning of November 10, 1978, was something he'd seen only on the screen of his television. The picturesque scene reminded him of a Winter Olympics venue: the sun glistening on snow-covered peaks, the mountains framing a city full of rustic architecture.

"When you're a kid and you see snow, you want to go out and play in the snow and build snowmen," Ivery said. "It's no different being a young man playing football in it for the first time. You want to get in that experience one time in your life, just to see what it's all about."

Georgia Tech's game against the Air Force Academy the next day would be the first of many Ivery would play in frigid conditions. The Green Bay Packers would draft him the following spring, and he would spend nine years plowing—for yardage—at Lambeau Field.

But his initiation to frozen tundra came at Falcon Stadium. And for Ivery the first time was the best. The senior tailback rushed for a then-NCAA record 356 yards the next afternoon, leading Tech to a 42–21 victory. The victory earned the Yellow Jackets their first national ranking in more than seven years and assured them their first bowl trip since 1972.

Every Georgia Tech player and coach on the airplane knew the Air Force game was the Jackets' best chance at reaching bowl eligibility. They were to play Notre Dame and Georgia—both top-fifteen teams—in the two games following Air Force. Tech's seniors, including Ivery, wanted to play in a bowl game before their careers ended, and beating the Falcons would take the pressure off the Jackets for the last two games.

Eddie Lee Ivery runs for yardage.

Yet as the charter touched down at the airport, none of that mattered. What looked surreal from the sky was miserable on the ground. Snow fell like confetti at a pep rally, and a cold wind cut through multiple layers of wool. Unfortunately for Tech's southern boys, the invention of Gore-Tex was years away.

They ran from the plane to the terminal and from the terminal to the bus that would take them to the hotel. Those sprints revealed the other atmospheric phenomenon Ivery would have to contend with the next day: altitude. Colorado Springs is 7,000 feet above sea level, compared with Atlanta at 1,200 feet. Any physical activity left him gasping for breath.

The conditions troubled head coach Pepper Rodgers. His team had never played in the snow or in subfreezing temperatures. What's more, the Yellow Jackets' offense was based almost entirely around Ivery. Rodgers had scrapped the wishbone in favor of an I-formation prior to the 1978 season, intent on getting Ivery more carries. "Eddie was the only reason for the switch," Rodgers said. "It was strictly because of him. In the best sense of the game the I-formation is not anywhere as near as good an offense as the wishbone. But Eddie Lee was special. He was good enough to make it work."

With the offense centered around Ivery, Tech's success was incumbent upon his running strong. If he couldn't catch his breath and had to sit out plays, Tech's offense would struggle. And against a ball-control team like Air Force, that could prove disastrous. The Yellow Jacket defense would spend too much time on the field.

Pregame conditions only heightened Rodgers's fears. The temperature dropped to around twenty degrees that afternoon, and a 20-mph wind blew through the stadium. "It was the coldest I'd ever been," backup quarterback Gary Lanier said. Groundskeepers brought in a street sweeper to blow snow off the turf twice before kickoff. "When I first went out for warm-ups, I was getting upset because I didn't think we would play the game in those conditions," Ivery said. "I wanted to play because I'd never played in conditions like that. It was snowing heavily. It was cold, but it wasn't like any other cold weather I would play in again."

The agitation that Ivery felt manifested itself later. By kickoff his stomach was churning. He had eaten a plate of eggs for breakfast, just as he did on most game days. Scramble those eggs with freezing temperatures, high altitude, and stress, however, and Ivery had a nausea omelet.

But as with basketball's Michael Jordan, illness sharpened Ivery's focus. The field was so slick that *Atlanta Journal-Constitution* sportswriter David Davidson would write in his game story the next day that "ice skates would have been more appropriate footwear than cleated shoes."

Ivery broke his first big run in the second quarter for a 73-yard touchdown. He celebrated by vomiting on the sidelines, overcome by his sour stomach. "I think it had a lot to do with the altitude," Ivery said. "Having never been in that before, after eating and then going out there and running in that type of atmosphere, it made me sick."

There was plenty of illness on Air Force's sideline as well. The Falcon defense could not stop Georgia Tech's rushing attack. Even when Ivery's stomach forced him to leave the game, his backups ran for yardage. Tech finished the day with 510 yards on the ground, with Ray Friday running for 115 yards on five carries and Darish Davis picking up 73 yards on six carries.

For all the yardage the Yellow Jackets failed to build a big lead. They led 14–3 at halftime, and Ivery's status was in doubt. The trainers made him force down a cup of Pepto-Bismol at halftime. That calmed his stomach long enough for him to pick up 124 yards in the third quarter. Ivery gained 80 yards on a touchdown run, following the blocking of tackle Ken Hill down the sideline on a toss sweep.

Air Force kept pace, however. Quarterback Dave Ziebart and wide receiver Cormac Carney were doing through the air what Ivery was doing on the ground. Ziebart threw for 281 yards in the game, with Carney catching eleven balls for 204 yards. And by the end of the third quarter, they had cut Georgia Tech's lead to 28–21. "We had to gain as many yards as we did to win the football game," Ivery said. "Every time we scored, they'd come right back and score."

The Jackets finally pulled away in the fourth quarter. Ivery scored his third touchdown of the day early in the period, a 57-yard run that put him over the 300-yard mark. Friday added a 66-yard scoring run on the next possession to give Tech a 42–21 lead.

Ivery didn't see Friday's clincher. He was back on the sidelines retching his guts out. He'd opened the possession in the backfield, breaking a long run that brought him within 15 yards of the single-game rushing record of 351 yards held by Michigan State's Eric Allen. His upset stomach forced him to leave the game, and Friday's touchdown run came on the next play.

Georgia Tech's coaches knew Ivery was nearing the record. Rodgers put him back into the game on the next possession, and he promptly broke off a 21-yard run to surpass Allen's mark. He fumbled at the end of the run, though, and Air Force recovered, setting off a moment of panic among Tech's coaches. They called up to the press box to make sure the lost fumble didn't nullify the yards.

Eddie Lee Ivery (40) dodges Air Force tacklers during his record-breaking 1978 game.

It didn't. The yards counted. Rodgers put his second-team offense in the next time Tech got the ball back but only after debating with Ivery about going for 400 yards. Rodgers recounted the conversation with Ivery. "Go back in there and get 44 yards and make it even 400," Rodgers told Ivery. "If you pop a long one, just fall down when you get to 44."

Davidson's newspaper account quotes safety Don Bessil-lieu, who was eavesdropping on Rodgers, as saying, "Don't do it. You never know, you might lose some yards." Ivery wouldn't have, Lanier said. "I can remember so many games getting in that huddle and calling his number and looking in his eyes," said Lanier. "He'd been beaten and beaten and beaten, and you're wondering, 'Is he going to be able to make it? Can he run it one more time?' He always did." But Ivery stayed on the sideline. And on the opening play of the next possession, Friday ran for 40 yards.

"I easily could have done it. I kind of internally said to myself, 'Man, you could have gotten 400,'" Ivery said. "The most important thing, obviously, was to win the game. Once they saw I was close to the record, they did let me go out there and shoot for it. I don't believe to this day that if I hadn't gotten that record on that first series he would have put me back out there."

Ivery's final numbers: twenty-six carries, 356 yards, three touchdowns. The performance is still the best in Georgia Tech history, and two of his runs in the game rank among the top-ten longest ever at the school. Ivery would go on to finish with 1,562 yards on the season, another Yellow Jacket record.

Ivery's national single-game record would stand for six years before Washington State's Rueben Mayes rushed for 357 yards against Oregon. LaDainian Tomlinson is the only player to rush for over 400 yards in a game, gaining 406 for Texas Christian in 1999. Ivery's performance ranked as the eleventh best all-time as of the end of the 2005 season. "You hear about people being in one of those zones," Ivery said. "That was the frame of mind I was in. I was in the zone."

Some will always remember Ivery's being in the zone. Fans often tell him the Air Force game defined his football career. He disagrees. Ivery's personal defining moment came fifteen years later—on a single run. He didn't have to elude any tacklers or defeat a defensive scheme geared toward stopping him. In fact, he walked. But his dash up the aisle at Georgia Tech's 1992 commencement ceremonies was the longest and hardest of his life to that point.

"A lot of my people back home didn't believe I could come to a school like Georgia Tech and play football and graduate," Ivery said. "I first heard that the day I committed. And I heard it every time I went back. For fifteen years I heard it."

Ivery was one of the first black football players at Georgia Tech. The state's public schools were integrated when he was in junior high, and the first Tech team to include several black players took the field in 1974, the year before Ivery arrived. He originally committed to play at Georgia. Coach Vince Dooley had built the Bulldog program into a national power, and Georgia offered a less rigorous academic curriculum than Tech. Ivery was a coveted recruit: He rushed for 1,700 yards in just ten games for Thomson in 1974.

Days before Ivery was to sign a letter of intent and accept Georgia's scholarship offer, however, Georgia Tech's Dick Bestwick visited Thomson. Bestwick was Rodgers's offensive line coach and one of his top recruiters. He pulled Ivery out of a math class on a Friday afternoon and made his last pitch to Ivery. And what a pitch it was. He told Ivery that Ivery

0-for-Georgia

Frustration brought tears to Eddie Lee Ivery's eyes during the last regular-season game of his Georgia Tech career. An ankle sprain forced Ivery out of the Yellow Jackets' 1978 loss to Georgia, arguably the greatest game in the century-old rivalry.

Tech led 28–21, and Ivery had 160 yards rushing and a touchdown when he suffered the injury in the final minute of the third quarter. He went to the sideline and got his ankle retaped, but he couldn't run on it and did not return to the game.

"That was the saddest point of my career," Ivery said. "Seeing Georgia get the momentum and go ahead of us while sitting on the sidelines knowing there was nothing I could do to help my teammates out brought tears to my eyes."

Georgia rallied behind freshman quarterback Buck Belue, who would go on to a storied career with the Bulldogs. He replaced starter Jeff Pyburn early in the second quarter with Georgia trailing 20–0. Belue led the deciding touchdown drive midway through the fourth quarter. He threw a 43-yard touchdown pass to Anthony Arnold on a fourth-down play with three minutes left. That pulled Georgia to within a point, and coach Vince Dooley decided to go for two. Belue threw an incompletion on the conversion but got a second chance thanks to a pass-interference call. A yard closer to the end zone, Georgia converted to take a 29–28 lead.

Tech's offense finally found a rhythm without Ivery in the closing minutes. The Jackets drove down inside the Georgia 40 yard line before the Bulldogs' David Archer, a freshman like Belue , intercepted a pass to seal the game.

"This is no doubt one of the greatest wins in Georgia history," Dooley said after the game. "I've never had any team come back and stay in the game like this one."

The loss devastated Ivery. He never beat the Bulldogs in his Tech career. "You're always disappointed when you don't beat your arch rival. That's a game, you throw out all the other games you've played all year long, and when it comes down to that University of Georgia game, you want to win that game. Even if you win every game of the season or lose every game of the season, you want to win that one."

belonged at Tech. Yes, the academics were challenging. But they weren't insurmountable.

Bestwick told Ivery that if Ivery came to Tech, Bestwick would see to it that Ivery would graduate. "For the first time in my life, I saw some sincerity on a man who really cared for me as a human being," Ivery said. "He didn't just want me to come to school and play football. He cared for me as a person—a person he wanted to see graduate from Georgia Tech. That won me over."

Ivery failed to sell the notion of his going to Tech to his friends and neighbors quite so effectively. Most told him he'd never graduate. Many said he'd struggle to stay eligible. Some predicted he'd flunk out or be forced to transfer. He played four years instead and left Tech without a degree only because the Packers picked him in the first round of the 1979 draft.

But Ivery never stopped thinking about making his diploma run. Bestwick wouldn't let him. The coach left Tech following the 1975 season but, true to his word, kept up with Ivery. After Ivery's pro career ended following the 1986 season, Bestwick encouraged him to finish his education.

Bestwick was relentless, and Ivery finally returned to Tech in 1990. He was coaching Thomson at the time, and the National Consortium for Academics and Sports offered to pay for him to finish his schooling. Two years later he scored big, earning his degree in industrial management.

"That's what defined my career at Georgia Tech," Ivery said. "Dick Bestwick lived up to his word. From 1975 to 1989 he encouraged me to get that diploma. And all the critics back home who said I would never play football at Georgia Tech and graduate were answered. When I walked down the aisle and got that diploma, my Georgia Tech career was defined."

Defined but far from over. In the years that followed, life would do to Ivery what the Air Force defense couldn't: tackle him. And Georgia Tech would rally around him once again. By the mid-1990s football no longer defined Ivery. Drug and alcohol abuse did. He began a career with Russell Athletics after graduation but quit after six months. He moved his family back to Thomson and took up partying as his occupation.

The hometown hero couldn't hold down a job in his hometown. His addiction was so deep his wife moved with their two children to Florida in 1994 to escape him. That only worsened his condition. His downward spiral continued for four more years before he finally saw his reflection in the mirror one night and didn't recognize himself. He checked into an addiction-treatment center the next day.

Not long after, two men came to visit Ivery. One was Dave Braine, a Georgia Tech assistant coach during Ivery's playing days and now the school's athletic director; the other was Jack Thompson, a longtime Georgia Tech employee who'd known Ivery since Ivery was seventeen years old. The three shared lunch often at the treatment center. They talked about old times and new times, the good and the bad. They let Ivery know Georgia Tech had not forgotten about him.

And after Ivery completed the program and started his life over, they gave him a second chance. Ivery called Braine for advice on getting back into coaching. Braine hired him instead, giving him a position in Georgia Tech's strength and conditioning program.

"When you look at my career and see that God has given me the opportunity to come back and be a part of what I truly believe started my life out, it is so exciting to me," Ivery said. "It's amazing to me that my life has made a 360-degree turn—that I ended up back up at the place where I really got started.

"I went through a lot of bumps and bruises on the road to get here. By God's grace I'm here, and now I can share my experiences, both in football and in life."

The Miracle on the Flats

Gary Sisson started climbing. Up and up he climbed, to the top of the University of Virginia's Scott Stadium, up near the light standards. His son Scott followed him step for step. Scott had made history here years earlier, several hundred feet below on the playing field. They finally reached the top. This, Gary told his son, was where he sweated out the time-out that preceded the kick. "Our neighbor from back home was up there trying to talk him down," Scott said. "He said, 'You have no idea how much pressure there is watching you kick.'"

Scott Sisson made the kick, a 37-yard field goal in the closing seconds of Tech's game against number one Virginia on November 3, 1990. Those 3 points gave the Yellow Jackets a 41–38 upset victory. The kick was the most poignant moment in the unlikeliest of championship seasons. In college athletics there are Cinderellas—and there is the 1990 Georgia Tech football team.

The Yellow Jackets opened the season unranked. They hadn't cracked the national polls in more than five seasons, in fact. They hadn't been to a bowl game since 1985. The seniors were two years removed from a 3–8 season. As freshmen they'd gone 2–9, the only wins against the Citadel, a Division I-AA opponent, and Indiana State, a school recognizable only because Larry Bird had led its basketball team to the national championship game a decade earlier.

Yet with Sisson's kick, Georgia Tech became a national title contender. Pollsters had voted the Jackets into the top twenty-five five weeks earlier, and the Virginia upset moved them up to number seven with three weeks left in the regular season. They'd arrived, and they knew it. And they celebrated for hours. They lingered on the Scott Stadium sideline until after the stunned home crowd had filed out. Gary Sisson shared hugs with his son, having been successfully talked down from the nose-bleed section.

The party continued in the locker room. Players sprayed each other with sodas and danced around as if they'd just won the World Series. Coach Bobby Ross told his team, "We're back. We're finally back." The bash became more emotional when Bus Ross, the frail father of Tech's coach, addressed the team and was awarded a game ball. The celebrants were ankle deep in tears

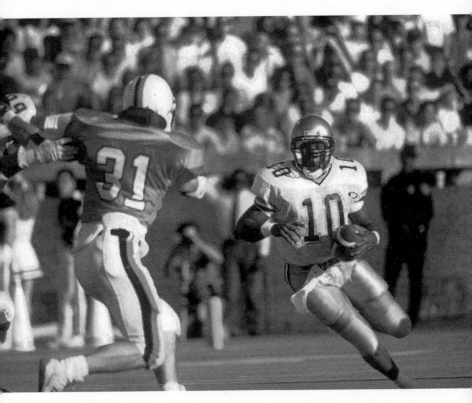

Quarterback Shawn Jones scrambles during the Yellow Jackets' upset of number one Virginia.

and sodas by the time they were to leave to catch their flight back home to Atlanta.

The bus ride to the airport and the flight were just as raucous as the locker-room scene. Players and coaches took turns dancing in the aisles. A welcoming committee of several hundred fans greeted them at the airport. They traded hugs and high-fives, reveling a little longer in the upset victory. As they boarded the buses for the short ride to campus, most fell silent. They were wiped out, "ready for bed," as offensive lineman Mike Mooney said. The game had drained them. The aftermath had finished them off.

Fullback William Bell realized that something more awaited them that night as the buses prepared to turn onto North Avenue just a few blocks east of campus. "People were cheering all along the street, at the BP [gas station] and the Varsity and places like that," Bell said. "I didn't realize everything was going on until we turned the corner on Techwood Drive."

Tech's student body met the buses on Techwood, which runs along the east side of Bobby Dodd Stadium. They'd been celebrating for hours. They stormed the empty stadium and tore down the goal posts, dragging them out into the street. They built a bonfire in an intersection, one that grew so hot it melted the traffic light overhead. As the buses turned into campus, the party began anew. "It was as if we had just won the Super Bowl," Bell said.

The reception shocked the team almost as much as their upset of Virginia had stunned the nation. Tech was decades removed from being a football school, and the team was used to pulling into campus anonymously from road games. "I remember turning the corner and thinking something else was going on," Mooney said. "I was like, 'What are all these people doing?'"

Mooney's linemate, Jim Lavin, considered the moment to be as significant as Sisson's kick earlier in the day. "I figured people would be in their dorm rooms studying as usual," Lavin said. "It was good to see people were excited about football. But you have to give them a reason to be. Give them reasons to get out of the library and out of the study halls."

Lavin and the rest of Tech's upperclassmen had begun their careers eliciting more jeers than cheers. The seniors and fifth-year players on the 1990 team had been recruited by Ross's predecessor, Bill Curry. Curry started a football renaissance at Tech in the mid-1980s. He coached the 1985 team to a 9–2–1 record and the All-America Bowl. One year later, after a 5–5–1 season, Curry left to coach at Alabama.

Georgia Tech turned to Ross. He had coached Maryland to three Atlantic Coast Conference titles in the 1980s only to abruptly resign following the 1986 season. Within days of Curry's accepting the Bama job, Tech hired Ross.

The contrasting coaching styles of Curry and Ross led to clashes with players. Ross was a graduate of Virginia Military Institute and took a disciplined, military-like approach to football. Many of the Curry holdovers openly defied Ross early on. Lavin says they almost drove him out of coaching. And the on-field performance reflected the internal strife.

Sisson recalls tagging along with a high school buddy on his recruiting visit to Tech in 1988. He was appalled by the Yellow Jackets' play. "They were horrible," Sisson said. "And the game I went to, they won."

The Jackets beat South Carolina 34–0 on October 15, 1988. It was their only win against a major college team in Ross's first two years. "I had no illusions of grandeur when I went there," Sisson said. "I just wanted to get a good education and be able to say I was a college kicker."

While Ross's early teams struggled on the field, the coach and his assistants were succeeding at recruiting. Ross was hired too late to do much in 1987, but his next class included Mooney,

All-America Ken Swilling casts his vote for number one following the win against Georgia.

defensive backs Ken Swilling and Willie Clay, and tight end Tom Covington. A year later he signed Bell, defensive tackle Coleman Rudolph, wide receiver Bobby Rodriguez, and linebacker Calvin Tiggle.

The 1988 class also included the two playmakers around whom coordinators Ralph Friedgen and George O'Leary would base their schemes: quarterback Shawn Jones and linebacker Marco Coleman. Jones had grown up in Thomasville, a small town near the Georgia-Florida border where the only event more cherished than a Friday night football game is a Sunday morning church service. Jones was overshadowed during his prep career by the county rival's quarterback, Thomas County Central's Charlie Ward.

Ward attended Florida State, where he would win the Heisman Trophy. Jones contemplated going to Georgia, but coach Ray Goff wouldn't promise him a chance to play quarterback. Ross did, so Jones went to Tech. He quarterbacked the scout team in 1988, taking a freshman redshirt. He had the mobility Friedgen coveted and moved to first team the following spring.

Coleman impressed as a scout-teamer as well. He stood 6'3" and carried his 240 pounds nimbly, making him almost unblockable in practice. He would leave Georgia Tech after his redshirt junior year and become the seventh first-round draft pick in school history.

The talents of Jones and Coleman helped spark a gradual turnaround in 1989. The Yellow Jackets opened the season with three straight losses as young players gained experience. The fourth week of the season was an open date on the schedule. Ross asked his assistants to evaluate each other—Friedgen and the

A Winning Combo

George O'Leary and Ralph Friedgen became close friends during their years working under Bobby Ross at Georgia Tech. They were even neighbors, driving in to work together most days. They reunited in 1997, when O'Leary hired Friedgen as the Yellow Jackets' offensive coordinator. They quickly rekindled the success they'd had as Ross's coordinators. The Jackets went 34–14 and won a share of the 1998 ACC title in their four years together back on the Flats.

Friedgen left Georgia Tech following the 2000 season to become the head coach at Maryland, his alma mater. The Terrapins won the ACC title his first year and won ten or more games each of his first three seasons.

O'Leary departed the Flats in 2001 to coach at Notre Dame, but an embellished résumé cost him his dream job. He returned to college coaching in 2004 at Central Florida, and after a winless first season, the Black Knights finished 8–4 in 2005 and won the Conference USA East Division title.

offensive coaches critiqued the defense, while O'Leary and his defensive assistants analyzed the offense. The exchanges resulted in altered strategies: The offense would run the option more to take advantage of Jones's mobility; the defense would focus on getting a better pass rush.

Maryland visited Atlanta the following Saturday, and Tech promptly fell behind 14–0. But in the final minute before halftime, Jones went from rookie to veteran. He marched the Yellow Jackets for a touchdown and kept it up in the second half as the Jackets won 28–24.

Georgia Tech went on to win six of its last seven games and finish 7–4. "It was very pivotal and crucial when we turned it around against Maryland at halftime," Lavin said. "We were a team without a whole lot of confidence. We had talent, lots of it. We just lacked confidence. It was very important to the psyche and confidence of the team."

So too was what happened the week after Tech capped its run with a win against archrival Georgia. Actually it was what *didn't* happen—a bowl invitation. "Getting snubbed out of a bowl made people a little bit hungrier," Lavin said. "Many people thought we had turned the corner. The disappointment over not making a bowl stayed with us the whole off-season."

Confidence and drive would not be a problem for Tech in 1990. Swilling predicted a perfect season just as fall practice was set to open. Several teammates thought it possible as well, although none voiced their feelings so publicly.

"We were talking national championship before the first day we walked in there," Mooney said. "We didn't talk to other people about it. They would have laughed at us. We had beaten Clemson at Clemson the year before. They were always a top-five, top-ten. The schedule kind of fell in our favor. Not going to a bowl game the year before was probably the best thing that ever happened to us as far as motivation going into the championship year."

The Yellow Jackets may have been dreaming of titles, but they had personnel issues to resolve first. Tailback Jerry Mays exhausted his eligibility while rushing for 1,349 yards in 1989.

Bell, a sophomore who had carried just seventeen times the year before, replaced Mays in the backfield. On defense O'Leary lost his entire line. He plugged in senior Jeremiah McClary and two sophomores. If they didn't perform up front, the linebackers, primarily Coleman and Tiggle, would have to contend with blockers all season.

Bell proved a worthy successor to Mays, rushing for over 1,000 yards. And he had no doubts about the new defensive line's abilities, even if others did. "When you practice against those guys, you know they're good," Bell said. "I didn't realize I was practicing against all-conference guys, of course. After a couple of games, I realized the things they were doing at practice, wreaking all that havoc, wasn't a reflection on our offense. They actually did better against our opponents than they did against us."

Bell's realization took a few weeks because Georgia Tech's defense needed time—and game experience—to mesh. Tech fell behind North Carolina State 10–0 in the opener before Jones led a rally. The Yellow Jackets drilled Tennessee-Chattanooga the next week, forcing seven turnovers. But Ross told the media afterward he expected better play from the defense.

He got it a week later against undefeated South Carolina in a game shown nationally on ESPN. Georgia Tech held the Gamecocks to 196 yards, including 40 on the ground, and forced five turnovers in a 27–6 shellacking. The next day voters elected Tech to the national rankings: eighteenth in the Associated Press writers' poll and twenty-third in the United Press International coaches' poll.

The next week Coleman became an All-America candidate by sacking Maryland's highly touted quarterback, Scott Zolak, five times in a 31–3 victory. The win upped the Yellow Jackets' record to 4–0, the program's best start since 1970. The defense had yet to allow a touchdown all season and ranked among the nation's top-five teams in points allowed, total yards allowed, rushing yards allowed, and turnover margin.

Clemson loomed next on Georgia Tech's schedule, though. The Tigers owned the ACC at the time. Florida State wouldn't join the conference until 1992. Coach Danny Ford guided Clemson to six ACC titles in the 1980s and won the 1981 national championship. Yet Tech teams always seemed to play well against their closest ACC neighbor. Clemson is located two hours northeast of Atlanta along Interstate 85, a couple dozen miles the other side of the South Carolina border. The Yellow Jackets officially joined the ACC in 1983 and beat Clemson in 1984, 1985, and again in 1989.

The Tigers had a new coach in 1990: Ken Hatfield, a highly successful coach first at Air Force and then at Arkansas. Hatfield was a master of the option offense from his days at Air Force and a believer in the hard-nosed defensive attitude favored by Arkansas and the other teams of the Southwest Conference.

Georgia Tech jumped out to a quick 14–0 lead nonetheless. A blowout failed to materialize, however. Clemson's option began to grind out yards and dominate the clock. The Yellow Jackets ran just eleven offensive plays in the second half as the Tigers trimmed the deficit to 14–12 by the opening minute of the fourth quarter.

Every national championship team can point to a clutch play or two that saved its season. The 2005 Southern California team had the fourth-down pass from Matt Leinart to Dwayne Jarrett

Emmett Merchant catches a touchdown pass during the 21–19 victory over Clemson.

and the "Reggie Bush push" on the goal line, both in a win against Notre Dame. In 2002 Ohio State needed a fourth-down touchdown pass from Craig Krenzel to beat Purdue. Tennessee's Billy Ratliffe pounced on a fumbled snap by Arkansas quarterback Clint Stoerner that kept the Volunteers marching toward the 1998 title.

Georgia Tech had several such plays in 1990. Kick returner Kevin Tisdel made the first early in the fourth quarter of the Clemson game, returning a kickoff 87 yards to set up the deciding touchdown in the eventual 21–19 win. The Yellow Jackets moved to number eleven in the polls the next day. A victory the following Saturday against winless North Carolina would surely vault them into the top ten. But a loss would foil all their hopes.

The Jackets neither won nor lost. They tied. Georgia Tech played without three starters: Mooney didn't make the trip because of a hand injury; Swilling had hurt his foot the previous week and thus watched the game from the sidelines; and offensive tackle Russell Freeman—playing in Mooney's place—broke his wrist on the first series. Two other offensive linemen played through injuries. "I would have fought with them to go had I known Russell was going to get hurt right off the bat," Mooney said. "I listened to the game on the radio. It was probably the longest day of my life."

Tech missed the offensive linemen the most. Three drives stalled inside the 10 yard line, two right at the goal line. Normally the Jackets would run the ball behind Mooney in those situations. Without him or Freeman they scored just 6 points on those three drives. "It felt like a loss to me," said Lavin, who wept in the locker room afterward. "We didn't get the job done. That was on us. It was the lowlight of the year."

The tie lit the way to the rest of the season, however. Winning is as dangerous as it is contagious to a team not accustomed to it. Overconfidence comes too easily. The tie was a relatively harmless reality check for the Jackets, keeping their championship hopes alive while forcing them to refocus on the opponents ahead. Georgia Tech rebounded from the tie to hammer Duke 48–31 the next week and improve to 6–0–1. Next up: Virginia. Top-ranked and led by the Moores—quarterback Shawn and wide receiver Herman—the Cavaliers averaged 48 points and 550 yards a game.

Someone else burned up the field before the Cavs' offense got its chance. Vandals broke into the stadium the night before the game and set a portion of the artificial turf on fire. The grounds crew patched the spot in time for kickoff, though.

Virginia's offense took over where the vandals left off, jumping out to a 13–0 lead. The Yellow Jackets' secondary couldn't cover Herman Moore. He finished the day with nine catches for 234 yards and a touchdown. The Cavaliers stretched the lead to 28–14 by halftime. "That was one game where if the defense was on the field, you stood up and watched," Bell said. "Other games, you come to the sideline, you sit down on the bench and rest. But their offense was so good you caught your breath as quick as you could and then stood up and watched. But we didn't get rattled."

Just the opposite. Georgia Tech rallied coming out of the locker room. Tiggle recovered a fumble on the opening play of the second half. Jones turned the takeaway into a touchdown. On Virginia's ensuing possession, Tiggle intercepted a pass. Tech didn't score off that turnover, but the momentum had swung.

The Yellow Jackets tied the game at 28 late in the third quarter. Virginia retook the lead 35–28 on the next possession. The Jackets answered with a touchdown drive of their own.

That's when Gary Sisson started his climb. Scott Sisson gave Tech its first lead minutes later with a 32-yard field goal. The Moores drove Virginia again, but a penalty nullified a touchdown pass, and Tiggle tipped away another throw intended for Herman Moore in the end zone. They settled for a field goal.

Tech was about to get the ball in a tie game with 2:34 left. Bell was smiling on the Tech sideline, sensing victory. Jones would drive the Jackets into field goal range, and Sisson would kick the game-winner. "I don't know if Scott understood that even before he kicked it, we knew we had won the game," Bell said. "When we got into field goal range, we just assumed. We just assumed it was automatic." It was. Sisson's 37-yarder came with just seven seconds left, too little time even for Shawn and Herman Moore. Tech had pulled the upset.

Sisson kicked two more field goals the next week—including the game-winner with eight seconds left—as the Yellow Jackets survived a scare against Virginia Tech. They finished with convincing wins against Wake Forest and Georgia. At 10–0–1 Georgia Tech was ranked second in the country behind Colorado. How the Buffaloes were number one will go down as one of the great mysteries in college football history. Their record was 9–1–1, including a win that shouldn't have been.

Colorado played Big 8 Conference rival Missouri on October 6, 1990. Trailing 31–27, the Buffaloes drove down to the 1 yard line in the closing seconds. Missouri stuffed tailback Eric Bieniemy on a third-down play, but officials stopped the clock with eight seconds left because Missouri's player weren't unpiling fast enough.

Coach Bobby Ross is carried off the field after a Yellow Jackets victory.

As the officials spotted the ball and signaled for the clock to resume running, Colorado quarterback Charles Johnson looked at the sideline down marker. It read "third down" instead of "fourth down." The official had forgotten to change it after second down. Johnson spiked the ball to stop the clock. The referee didn't realize the mistake. Instead of awarding Missouri possession, he gave Colorado another down. Johnson scored on a quarterback sneak on the extra play, and the Buffaloes won 34–31. To this day the game is known as Colorado's "fifth-down win."

As controversial as the victory was that day, it become downright dubious as New Year's Day approached. Colorado received

Georgia Tech's defense recovers a fumble in the Citrus Bowl win against Nebraska.

the Big 8's Orange Bowl bid as a result and played Notre Dame, while Tech took the ACC champion's spot in the Citrus Bowl against Nebraska.

Coach Bobby Ross poses with the national championship trophy.

Both teams won. Georgia Tech trounced the Cornhuskers 45–21. Colorado survived courtesy of a penalty flag that wiped out Notre Dame's Rocket Ismail's game-winning punt return for a touchdown. The next morning before the final polls were released, Sisson did an interview on national radio. On the other line was a Colorado player. "I was trying to be diplomatic, saying all the right things," Sisson said. "And the Colorado guy gets on there and starts ripping us. Saying how we didn't belong."

The coaches voting in the UPI poll disagreed. Tech won by one vote. Colorado, meanwhile, won the AP vote. The two teams were co-national champions. The Yellow Jacket players were ecstatic and disappointed at the same time. "We were the only team that had no losses," Lavin said. "Everybody remembers that Colorado had five downs. There's not a whole lot of absolutes in sports: four downs in football, three outs in baseball, and that's about it. So to me, there's no debate."

For some Yellow Jackets the debate would rage for years. Mooney went on to an NFL career after college and played on the same San Diego Chargers team as Colorado's Bieniemy. The two spent hours arguing over the title. "Bieniemy's big thing was they were in the Big 8, and they played a tougher schedule. They didn't. We played more ranked teams," Mooney said. "I don't blame Colorado, but I know we would have beaten them."

Sisson debated similar points with teammate and Colorado product Mitch Burger when both played for the Vikings. "We laughed about it," Sisson said. "It was water under the bridge.

"But everybody knows which team was better."

In-State Hate

The best advice a newcomer to Georgia can heed is never get in the middle of a Georgia Tech–Georgia debate. College football has its share of great rivalries, from Army-Navy and Ohio State–Michigan to Texas-Oklahoma and USC–Notre Dame. But when it comes to real bitterness, the in-state feuds, such as Auburn-Alabama, Clemson–South Carolina, Texas A&M–Texas, and Georgia Tech–Georgia, trump the rest.

Tech's First Field General

Dig deeply enough in a United States history book, and you should find the name of General Leonard Wood. His life is a footnote to several major events at the turn of the twentieth century: He led the military unit that captured the Apache Indian leader Geronimo; commanded the Rough Riders in the Spanish-American War along with his second-in-command, Teddy Roosevelt; and ran for president in 1920, losing the Republican nomination to Warren Harding. In the history of the Georgia Tech–Georgia football rivalry, Wood will never be overshadowed. He led Tech to a 28-6 victory in the inaugural game of the series in 1893.

Wood came to Atlanta in 1893 as the surgeon-general at Fort McPherson, located southwest of downtown. He had spent the years since capturing Geronimo living in California, where his favorite activity was playing football for the Olympic Club.

Needing a football fix, the army lieutenant with a doctorate of medicine rode his horse up to the Tech campus and enrolled as an undergraduate— and joined a one-year-old winless football team as player-coach. The Georgia Tech team went 0–3 in 1892, losing to Mercer, Vanderbilt, and Auburn.

Georgia Tech fans and Georgia fans have been hurling ill will at one another for more than 120 years now. The Bulldogs cast the first stone—literally—in the inaugural game between the two schools in 1893. Georgia Tech won the first meeting 28–6 in Athens, and Georgia fans reacted by slinging clods of dirt at the visitors throughout the closing minutes of the game.

The addition of Wood made the team much more formidable, though. Tech scheduled Georgia for its season opener in 1893, traveling to Athens to play at Herty Field. According to newspaper accounts, Tech's roster featured several other atypical undergrads in addition to Wood. Park Howell, a medical student, and John Kimball, an Atlanta attorney, also played for Tech.

Wood, a fullback, constituted most of Georgia Tech's offense. He scored the game's first touchdown and led two other scoring drives. He also took a rock to the forehead from an angry Georgia fan during the second half but remained in the game.

Tech played three more games that fall and finished with a 2–1–1 record, the first winning mark in school history. Wood coached and played at Georgia Tech again in 1894, but the team went 0–3, including a season-ending loss to a team from Wood's army base, Fort McPherson.

The Spanish-American War broke out in 1898, and Wood served in Cuba and would later become governor-general of Cuba and the Philippines. He kept up with Georgia Tech football, however, even as he rose to become the army's chief of staff and a presidential candidate.

Wood died in 1927 at the age of fifty-six, one year before Georgia Tech's momentous national championship season.

One of the dirt clods contained a rock, and it hit Tech's player-coach, thirty-three-year-old army surgeon Leonard Wood, in the brow. He wiped the blood away and remained in the game. The stoning persisted, though. "After the game, we were greeted by a shower of rocks, sticks, and missiles," Tech halfback Will Hunter told a news reporter at the time.

The incident has proven to be an omen in the century since. Although the rivalry has become more civilized, the passion remains. Fans of both schools openly mock each other. The favorite chant of Tech fans is "To hell with Georgia." Tech doesn't even have to be playing its rivals for the chant to come ringing out of the stands. A boring game or long time-outs can bring it on, no matter the opponent. The Bulldog faithful, meanwhile, sing "And to hell with Georgia Tech" as part of the school's fight song, "Glory to Old Georgia," set to the tune of "Battle Hymn of the Republic."

Teams from the two schools have met every season since 1925, and the feud is now fought annually on the Saturday after Thanksgiving, the final regular-season game on both their schedules. The date is about all the two schools agree on.

Depending on which team's media guide you look at, the 2005 game between Georgia Tech and Georgia was either the one hundredth meeting (Georgia Tech) or the ninety-eighth meeting (Georgia). The Bulldogs refuse to acknowledge Georgia Tech's victories in 1943 and 1944. Most of Georgia's players were away fighting World War II during the time, while the Yellow Jackets still fielded competitive teams in large part because of an influx of Navy sailors—the majority of them athletically gifted—placed at the Atlanta school for training by the government. Dan Magill, upon his hiring as Georgia's publicity director in 1948, told Bulldog coach Wally Butts he would no longer count the games among the series record.

"They were not true Georgia–Georgia Tech games," Magill told Loran Smith for his book *Wally's Boys*. "The players Tech had were not Tech men, they were outsiders who had initially enrolled to play football at other colleges."

Pepper Rodgers (left) talks with Georgia head coach Vince Dooley. Rodgers beat Dooley in their first meeting but lost the next five games against the Bulldogs.

With or without Tech's two World War II shutouts, the series remains among the most colorful in college football. Close games, season-spoiling upsets, and streaks both famous and infamous litter the results, and the game's outcome can make or break a season. Tech's legendary coach Bobby Dodd, who oversaw an eight-year winning streak against the Bulldogs that Georgia fans refer to simply as "the Drought," said defeating the rival was the key to keeping the fans happy.

"Any time you beat Georgia and win a bowl game, you had a great season," Dodd said in his biography, *Dodd's Luck*. "Don't make a difference what you did against Florida or Kentucky or Duke, they forget those things. They remember that Georgia game and that bowl game. That was big stuff."

Most years, the games are closely contested. Georgia Tech and Georgia tied five times prior to the institution of the overtime rule in the 1990s. Thirty-nine of the meetings were decided by 7 points or less, fourteen by 3 points or less, and six by a single point.

Many of the games turned on the strangest of plays, like extra points and two-point conversions. Tech tied Georgia 6–6 in 1937 when the Bulldogs' halfback/kicker Bill Hartman returned the second-half kickoff 93 yards for a touchdown but was too tired to kick the point. His backup missed the PAT after a bad snap. Twelve years later Georgia's kicker missed another extra point, this time giving Tech a 7–6 victory and starting "the Drought." Eleven years after that, Georgia's Pat Dye avenged that loss, blocking an extra point for a 7–6 Bulldog victory in Butts's last regular-season game as the Dogs coach. Dye also batted away a field goal try earlier in the game.

The 1978 game was decided on a two-point conversion. In that game Georgia quarterback Buck Belue began a career beloved by the Bulldog faithful, coming off the bench in the second quarter with his team trailing 20–0. Belue, then a freshman, would rally Georgia to a 29–28 victory, throwing a touchdown pass on fourth down with less than three minutes left to pull the Bulldogs within one. The Dogs went for two. Belue threw an incomplete pass, but the officials whistled Tech for pass interference. Georgia converted the second chance for a 29–28 victory.

A penalty flag helped decide the 1999 game as well. The two teams combined for over 1,000 yards and nearly 100 points, but the officiating crew likely played the biggest role in the game's outcome. With the game tied 48–48, Georgia drove down inside Tech's 5 yard line in the final minute. Looking to drain as much time off the clock as possible, Bulldog coach Jim Donnan decided to run another play on third down before sending his kicker in for the game-winning field goal. Tailback Jasper Sanks lost the ball as he hit the ground on the play, though, and Tech's Chris Young recovered. The Southeastern Conference officiating crew awarded Tech the ball, even as television replays showed Sanks was down when he fumbled.

Yellow Jacket kicker Luke Manget won the game in overtime with a 38-yard field goal, the kick coming after Georgia blocked his first attempt. Georgia Tech coach George O'Leary, unlike his counterpart Donnan, sent his kicker in on third down. The Bulldogs blocked that try, but Tech holder George Godsey recovered the ball. Manget's second attempt was true. "There have been so many great games, so many close games between the two," said Eddie Kilpatrick, a lifelong Tech fan from Savannah, Georgia. "You can't help but get caught up in it all."

The rivals also show a penchant for getting in each other's way. One has spoiled the other's national title hopes four times, going back to 1915. Georgia played John Heisman's Tech team to a scoreless tie on November 15, 1915, the only blemish on the Golden Tornado's record that season. One of Heisman's assistants that day, Bill Alexander, sullied an undefeated Georgia season twelve years later. The 1927 Bulldogs, nicknamed the

Luke Manget kicked the game-winning field goal in the 1999 Georgia–Georgia Tech game.

"Dream and Wonder" team by the media, shut out six of their first nine opponents before coming to Atlanta for the season finale. They met a Georgia Tech team well-rested and prepped for the game courtesy of "the Plan." Alexander split his team into two squads a month before the game. One of them, comprised mainly of reserves, played the three games prior to the Georgia game. The other, which included the usual starters, spent those four weeks practicing and scouting Georgia.

The Bulldogs' signature play that season was a dump screen pass over the offensive line. Tech stuffed it all day and blanked the Dogs 12–0, costing them a Rose Bowl trip.

The Tech-Georgia showdown with the biggest stakes came in 1942. The victor won the Southeastern Conference title and a bid to the Rose Bowl to play UCLA for the national championship. Georgia featured Charley Trippi and Frank Sinkwich in the backfield and was favored because Tech's star halfback, Clint Castleberry, was hurt and coach Alexander had suffered a heart attack midway through the season.

Alexander proved prophetic the day before the game, when he met with Edwin Camp, a sportswriter for the *Atlanta Journal*. "We are in for a bad day . . . The team is shot." Alexander told Camp. Georgia ripped Tech 34–0.

Dodd coached the Yellow Jackets that day in Alexander's absence, Dodd's first game as head coach in the rivalry. Dodd posted a winning record against the hated Dogs, but twenty-four years after that first loss, he departed the series in much the same agonizing way. His 1966 team, undefeated and a victory over the Bulldogs away from playing for a national title, lost 23–14 in Athens.

Overshadowing Dodd's bookend losses in the rivalry is his

eight-year win streak, the longest in series history. In Tech lore the victories stretched the length of what is referred to as "the Golden Era" on the Flats. At Georgia the string of defeats is known as "the Drought."

Tech has had some dry spells of its own during the rivalry. Dooley beat Tech his first five years at Georgia, including the final three years of Dodd's tenure. The Bulldogs won six straight years from 1978 to 1983, beginning with Belue's breakout game and spanning the Herschel Walker years, and seven straight starting in 1991.

The bitterness between the two schools is not confined to between the hedges in Athens or the bricks that wall the sidelines of Grant Field, however. Wins and losses might make a rivalry, but a feud requires something more: hate. The hate started just before the dirt and rocks flew in the 1893 game. Georgia Tech adopted one of Georgia's original school colors, gold, for the game. Two years earlier Bulldog football coach Dr. Charles Herty had removed gold from his team's uniforms because of its similarity to yellow, a cowardly color in Herty's opinion.

The Tech team further earned its stoning that afternoon by inviting 200 women from the all-female Lucy Cobb Institute, each of them decked out in white and gold, to cheer for Tech at the game. The Lucy Cobb campus was located in Athens, a little more than a mile from the playing field. The incident wounded the Bulldogs so deeply the tale is still recounted in the Georgia football media guide under the heading SCHOOL COLORS, STOLEN GIRLFRIENDS, AND YELLOW JACKET TREACHERY. The two teams didn't play again until 1897.

The series would be interrupted for an extended period only

once more, although the next dispute wouldn't be over uniform colors or young ladies. The United States entered World War I in 1917, and Georgia lost enough players to enlistment and the draft that it disbanded its football program for two seasons. Tech continued to play, though, winning a national championship in 1917 and posting a 6–1 record in 1918.

The war ended in 1918, and many soldiers returned to school that winter. Tech and Georgia scheduled two baseball games against each other in the spring of 1919, the first in Atlanta and the second in Athens. Tech's freshman students pulled a prank during their team's home game, sneaking around in the crowd and snatching the hats off the heads of Georgia fans.

By the time Tech traveled to Athens on May 17, 1919, Georgia's students had concocted their own practical joke. The Bulldogs won the game that day and celebrated with a victory parade. A fake tank with the words GEORGIA IN ARGONNE led off, immediately followed by a small car ridden in by three students dressed in Tech sweaters and holding a sign reading 1917 TECH IN ATLANTA. The parade line also included a female Georgia student dressed in yellow-patch clothing, as well as a light-skinned mule; a printed program passed out to parade watchers described the horse as, "a spirited quadruped as shown by its color [yellow]."

Tech responded to the shenanigans by severing relations with its rival for the next six years. The school even denied Georgia's request to play a game against Dartmouth in 1921 at Grant Field, where the Bulldogs often played home games in the first half of the twentieth century.

The series resumed in 1925, and the two teams have met

Georgia Tech students celebrate the 1999 overtime win against Georgia by tearing down the goalposts.

every year since. The disgruntlement continued, however, particularly after the Georgia board of regents moved the business program from Tech to Georgia in the 1930s. For years Tech's commerce school had allowed coaches Heisman and Alexander to recruit players not inclined to engineering as business majors.

Georgia's coach Butts further used Tech's curriculum against the Yellow Jackets in recruiting during the 1940s and 1950s. Each Tech student had to pass a calculus course, and when Butts would visit a recruit coveted by both schools, the coach would bring along a copy of a calculus text. "Can you pass this?" became a part of his recruiting pitch. In his biography Dodd recounted how he often would see the calculus book left by Butts when he conducted a home visit of a recruit.

Today Georgia is supported more loudly around the state than the Yellow Jackets. That's due partly to the disparity in the number of alumni between the schools. As of the 2004–05 school year, Georgia had three times as many graduates living in the state as Tech. And according to Yellow Jacket player Reggie Ball, football fans who didn't go to either school often relate better to the Bulldogs. "I think they see Georgia Tech as more the educational school, that it's like the nerd school, I guess."

One Tech grad and fervent Yellow Jacket fan admits Ball might be right, although the Jackets have more support around the state than folks realize.

"A Georgia fan will wake up on Saturday, paint himself black, and put a Bulldog flag on his car just to drive down to the local sports bar," said Ryan Martin, a 2001 Tech graduate. "Tech fans are a little more, well, intelligent than that."

About the Author

Adam Van Brimmer has been a college football beat writer for ten years. He has been on the Georgia Tech beat for the past three years, covering Yellow Jackets football for the Morris Communications news bureau in Atlanta.

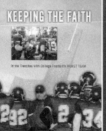 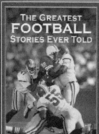